As a family man it hurts to ⋮
people. This book was desigr
dating process in a healthy ar.
keep the girl without compromising your values, then you need to go
"cop" this book.
 —Kirk Franklin
 Gospel Recording Artist

Sticky. Hurtful. Draining. Words like these should never describe a relationship. But the twenty-first-century's definition of dating has made it
so. Thankfully God has sent us Conway and Jada, lifelong friends of
mine whose integrity causes the message of this book to speak loud and
clear. Prepare to be challenged, convicted, and most important com-
pelled to be different as you prepare to embrace the relationships in a
way that brings God glory.
 —Priscilla Shirer
 Bible Teacher and Author

Sincere Christian singles are looking for a refreshing, practical, and godly
perspective on relationships. It's time for Christians to establish a
healthier norm for relationships to ensure a future with more Christ-
centered families. This book is a priceless and proven path to that end. I
have found great inspiration and encouragement through the wisdom
Conway and Jada offer, and it is a wonderful tool for discipling Christian singles.
 —Lekesha R. Barnett
 Assistant Pastor, New Faith Church, Houston, TX

Finally, my friend has put to paper a manual for dating and courting. In
2003, the words in this book were only thoughts that were passionately
communicated around a lunch table. If you're single, read it; if you're a
married, read it. Men, he calls us to lead, and lead we must! Buy this
book and read it, repeatedly!
 —Pastor Rick Cooper
 Associate Pastor of Married Couples & Single Adults
 North Dallas Community Bible Fellowship, Richardson, TX

When Love's in View is truly a thought-provoking and soul-stirring
book. This book discusses relationships in a way that is often felt by
most people but never, in truth, verbalized by anyone. It is remarkably

informative, yet astonishingly realistic; it gives real-life solutions to real-life struggles. Not only should every single person, both male and female, take the time to read this book, but every pastor or counselor of singles should read it. After reading the book, you will be equipped with the "antidote" on how to see a clearer picture of Christian "dating" and the roles that God destined for the man and woman.

—Eric L. Alexander, Senior Pastor
St. Luke Baptist Church, North Little Rock, AR

Every now and then, God gives you a friend that you instantly connect with at a deep level. Conway is one of those friends for me. His vulnerability opens the door for honest spiritual exploration, and his insight turns on the light of wisdom so that I can see my heart more clearly. More than anything, though, he helps me see Jesus' heart for me in the midst of my soul-searching. I have no doubt that as you read, he will do the same for you.

—Jeff Lawrence, Equipping Pastor
Northwest Bible Church, Dallas, TX

Guarding the heart is an ancient principle with modern applications. Conway and Jada take this principle and apply it to the fastest-growing population in America. Every unattached person would do well to ponder these principles and potentially save himself or herself a great deal of pain. You should seriously engage the principles of this book before you allow anyone else to engage your heart.

—James R. Womack, Senior Pastor
Destiny Church, Fort Worth, TX

Helen Keller was asked, "Do you know of anything that's worse than being blind?" She thought for a moment and then said, "Yes, there is one thing worse than being blind—having sight with no vision." Unfortunately my wife and I were once visionless college singles pursuing dating relationships by sight alone. Lacking a vision for singleness proved detrimental in much of our relational decision making as collegians. We needed a guide! It is with great delight that I endorse Dr. Conway and Jada Edwards, *When Love's in View: Finding Focus in Dating and Relationships*, as a progressive blueprint for guiding singles with real issues to the destination of healthy relationships.

—Rev. & Mrs. Curtis Woods
Kentucky State University, Campus Ministers

When Love's in View

finding focus in
dating and relationships

Dr. Conway and Jada Edwards

MOODY PUBLISHERS
CHICAGO

All Scripture quotations, unless otherwise indicated, are taken from the *New English Translation*. The NET Bible®, *New English Translation* Copyright © 1996 by Biblical Studies Press, L.L.C. NET Bible® is a registered Trademark. The NET Bible® Logo, Servicemark Copyright © 1997 by Biblical Studies Press, L.L.C. All rights reserved.

Scripture quotations marked AMP are taken from *The Amplified Bible*. Copyright © 1965, 1987 by The Zondervan Corporation. *The Amplified New Testament* copyright © 1958, 1987 by The Lockman Foundation. Used by permission.. (www.Lockman.org)

Scripture quotations marked NRSV are taken from the *New Revised Standard Version Bible,* copyright 1989, Division of Christian Education of the National Council of the Churches of Christ in the United States of America. Used by permission. All rights reserved.

Scripture quotations marked NIV are taken from the *Holy Bible, New International Version*®. NIV®. Copyright © 1973, 1978, 1984 by International Bible Society. Used by permission of Zondervan. All rights reserved.

Scripture quotations marked KJV are taken from the King James Version.

Editor: Kathryn Hall
Interior Design: Ragont Design
Cover Design and Image: Trevell Southall, TS Design
        www.tsdesignstudio.net (http://www.tsdesignstudio.net)

Library of Congress Cataloging-in-Publication Data
Edwards, Conway.
    When love's in view : finding focus in dating and relationships / Dr. Conway and Jada Edwards.
      p. cm.
    Includes bibliographical references.
    ISBN-13: 978-0-8024-8087-3
    ISBN-10: 0-8024-8087-X
    1. Single people—Religious life. 2. Single people—Conduct of life.
3. Single people—Sexual behavior. 4. Dating (Social customs)—Religious aspects—Christianity. I. Edwards, Jada. II. Title.

BV4596.S5E39 2008
248.8'4—dc22

                      2007034870

1 3 5 7 9 10 8 6 4 2

Printed in the United States of America

This book is dedicated to our parents,
who modeled the way.

contents

foreword

Many churches place so much emphasis on the state of marriage and family that often single men and women don't even think about the process or steps that might be necessary to achieve this end result. They also wonder whether or not it is possible to be single and satisfied. Well, I have good news for you: it is possible to be single and live a fulfilled life God's way. Otherwise, attempting to find satisfaction independent of God presents great danger because temptation to do so can lead to the opportunity for sin. That is, if you are single and unhappy in the role God has given you, you do not yet have a complete handle on God's kingdom view of singleness. Contentment with who you are can be a definite reality when you truly find your purpose in God.

Unfortunately, the church has often helped fuel a sense of incompleteness by its great emphasis on the family unit. There is nothing wrong with emphasizing the family, as this is also a necessary endeavor. But something is wrong with making singles feel like second-class citizens. Pastors often unconsciously fuel the discontent of single believers by helping them to simply cope with their status. But God doesn't want single people simply to cope. He wants them to flourish and succeed. Being single should not be a place of stagnation where men and women find themselves in a "holding pattern." Instead, it should be a season of life in which people are passionately pursuing God's call on their lives while being made ready to move in whatever direction He may lead them.

That's why it thrills me that one of my spiritual sons, Conway Edwards, along with his wife, Jada, who is like a daughter to me, have now written a guide for developing healthy relationships that prepares singles for lifelong, fulfilling marriages. For too long, we have allowed our culture and the world's affairs to influence our lives. Many singles today believe the Bible is silent on issues of dating, relationships, and courting, However, God has indeed spoken. In this God-inspired work, Conway and Jada use principles from the Word of God to help those who are unmarried get off the treadmill of unhealthy relationships and pursue responsible, healthy, God-honoring relationships.

This book provides single men and women, regardless of their age, a road map to follow in identifying, meeting, courting, and marrying God's best.

Dr. Tony Evans
Senior Pastor, Oak Cliff Bible Fellowship
President, The Urban Alternative

preface:
take the lead

One of our favorite movies is *Take the Lead,* directed by Liz Friedlander. Antonio Banderas portrays Pierre Dulaine, the real-life dance coach who tries to make a difference in the inner-city schools of New York. In his spare time, Pierre begins a class for children who may otherwise not have the opportunity to learn the art of dancing.

One of the aspects of the movie we liked most was how it used ballroom dancing as a great illustration of the manner in which a man is supposed to lead when engaging in dance with a woman. He must lead in a way that's graceful yet provides certainty and security. Moreover, the woman must be willing to follow him. The underlying principle in the movie is, if a man learns how to touch a woman with respect, such as through classical dance, then he is more likely to respect women in an overall sense. This is also true for women. If a woman knows how it feels to be touched with respect and led with grace, she might not let a guy treat her any other kind of way when it comes to relationships in general.

Men, our prayer is that you will lead courageously and graciously, fully embracing the incredible role that God has created for you. Women, our prayer is that you will expect good leadership from the men in authority in your lives and allow yourselves to respond positively to it.

Our hope in writing this book is that men and women will be encouraged to be content in their singleness and open to consider a God-inspired view on dating, love, and relationships. It is our prayer that something in this book will challenge every reader, whether single or married, to consider their present philosophy of dating and relationships, and evaluate it in light of the Word of God. In no way do we desire for this to be a legalistic manual on how to date and marry properly, but rather a valuable guide that will foster healthy, God-honoring relationships.

May you be consumed with God and His desires for your life. And while you are, may He give you the desires of your heart.

acknowledgments

For Jada and me, many people have shaped our thinking and our values. It takes a village to prepare, develop, and grow children for life as adults. But none are more critical than our parents. Between our parents there are more than seventy years of marriage. We want to thank Clyde and Barbara Edwards for their love for God and their commitment to each other. Their faith in God has been inspirational and motivational to us. We also want to thank James and Jean Cobon for their faithfulness to each other and the many sacrifices they have made to give Jada the best opportunity to succeed in life. We love you all.

Pastor Evans, thank you for being our pastor, a model, and a friend. Thank you for the privilege to serve under you in so many areas. Serving as the director of singles has been absolutely life-changing! Your commitment to excellence, your priority to family, and your love for both of us are greatly appreciated. Thanks so much for your life and your godly character.

To our singles ministry management team at Oak Cliff Bible Fellowship, thank you for the ride of our lives. Working with all of you has been exciting, challenging, and fulfilling. Thank you for the privilege to learn from you and grow with you. We bless you for the wonderful memories.

To our board of directors for Caribbean Choice for Christ in the United States and the board of directors for the National Centre for Christian Leadership Jamaica—thank you for believing in the vision of sharpening influencers to structure institutions that shape individuals with a Christocentric worldview.

We also want to thank our family and friends who helped us fine-tune this manuscript. To my (Conway's) sister Nicquet, thank you for taking the time to read and edit the book. To Adrienne, Angela, Anitra, Dianne, Mary, Racquel, Sonja, Tim, and Ty— thank you for your feedback and insight. To the great A.R., thank you for the time invested in designing the book.

introduction

Jada and I recently purchased a new camera. We called it an "investment" to justify spending a small fortune on something we can't drive, live in, or sit on. In all seriousness, this camera is the professional photographer's dream. It allows for a wide variety of photographic styles, and it has all of the capabilities we'll ever need and so much more. One of its features is the ability to switch between manual and automatic focus. We tried using the manual focus when we first purchased it because we wanted to look professional, which I'm sure we did.

The problem was that our pictures didn't turn out half as professional as *we* looked when taking them. Since those first attempts, we've decided to rely mainly on the automatic focus. However, we still actually use the manual focus first to determine the distance we want from our subject, and then we engage the auto focus to sharpen the image and determine whether we need a flash. It works splendidly! Our pictures of late have been great, and we still get to look a little bit like professionals.

Through this book we want to remind you that no matter where you may be in the dating process—or even if you haven't started—God is still the most important "subject" in your life, and He deserves your primary focus. To make this truth a reality for you, allow the Holy Spirit to be your "auto focus." If instead you rely on your own wisdom and strength to guide you, which we refer to as using a "manual focus," it will distract you from being aware of God's plan for your life. It is only when you center your focus on God that you will begin to see His perspective on dating and relationships more clearly. Prayerfully, this book will help you to see Him, yourself, and your relationships with new eyes of faith in God and know that He desires to give you His very best.

If you're not convinced that operating solely with manual focus can get you into trouble, think about these questions. Have you ever been involved in a breakup and asked yourself the standard questions about why the relationship ended? Have you ever spent a whole day, or even an entire month, going over whose fault it was? Have you ever thought that if you'd just done something more, perhaps you could have kept it together? In retrospect, you or the person you were dating probably tried doing things your way; that is, using your manual focus rather than including God in your decisions and actions regarding the relationship.

By looking at the statistics, it's apparent that most of us tend to favor doing things our way; this approach has by far been proven unsuccessful. In fact, it seems that our society as a whole is missing the mark in the arena of dating relationships. Let's take a look at what statistics reveal about first marriages. Based on 2000 census data, the Centers for Disease Control and Prevention reported that 20 percent of first marriages end within five years, 33 percent end within ten years, and 50 percent end within twenty years. For those in their second marriages, the statistics were worse. Approximately 54 percent of second marriages end within five years, 75 percent end within ten years, and 83 percent end within fifteen years. Overall, about 60 percent of all marriages eventually end in divorce. [1]

For this information to be meaningful to us, we need to open our eyes and look beyond the black-and-white data from the latest studies. What these numbers actually represent are shattered dreams, crushed hopes, and devastated hearts. Most people concede that these numbers are staggering statistics of failure, but not many seem to have solutions for this growing crisis. So allow me ask the question: how can we get this right? For the sake of our lives, our destinies in Christ, the ministries that God has entrusted to us, and the next generation coming after us—we must get this right.

Marital problems often stem from issues that grew out of the relationship initially formed during the dating stage. Moreover, problems that occur in dating relationships are often rooted in unresolved issues within the individuals. So if we are to start anywhere, we should begin with ourselves. We must first look at who God wants us to be as individuals and gauge how we're progressing on a personal basis before we can deal with the wider world of dating and relationships. Christians sometimes behave as though God has not spoken on the subject of dating, but nothing could be further from the truth. God's Word provides comprehensible insight and fundamental principles to help us approach relationships from a biblical perspective.

Now, I'll be the first to admit that I've not always applied these fundamental truths to my own life. As a matter of fact, this book was birthed from a search I embarked on after the embarrassing experience that I describe in chapter 1. I thank God for that season of my life, because the exploration I undertook changed my life forever. In these next few pages, I'll share with you what I discovered along this painful, powerful, and, above all, valuable journey with God.

As you read, I hope you will embark upon a journey that will enhance your own personal development. To better understand who you are becoming, your enlightenment must begin with discovering the fundamental roles God intends for men and women to possess. For too long we have misunderstood the core meaning of manhood and womanhood, and the devastating effects on our society are painfully obvious. Yet Jesus said, "You will know the truth, and the truth will set you free" (John 8:32).

It is my prayer that this book will help you discover the truth of God's Word about important principles for engaging in healthy relationships. We also hope that others will then be able to witness your success, choose to follow your godly example, and gain victory in their lives as well.

—CONWAY EDWARDS

1. Bramlett MD, Mosher WD. First marriage dissolution, divorce, and remarriage: United States. Advanced data from vital and health statistics; no. 323.Hyattsville, Maryland: National Center for Health Statistics, 2001. http://www.cdc.gov/nchs/data/ad/ad323.pdf.

the journey begins

This story began at a time in my life when God chose to teach me about spiritual maturity. You see, He was ready for me to grow in my character and went about capturing my attention in a very interesting way. I had been in America for about three years. I was pursuing my master's degree in business while serving as youth pastor for a church in San Diego, California. As far as I was concerned, life was wonderful. I was enjoying school, but most of all I enjoyed my role in ministering to young people. Little did I know—my life was about to drastically change.

One day while studying, a young lady ran up to me, crying. "You don't know me," she began, "but I know you. You're the youth pastor at our church. I just lost my thesis when the computer crashed. Could you pray for me?"

"I'd love to; let's pray," I replied. After all, I was a youth pastor at the church, and it was my duty to support any member during such an anxious time. That prayer began an interesting relationship between us. We started talking more at church, as well as spending time together outside of church. It wasn't too long before we became very good friends. She was a sweet young lady who loved ministry. We had great conversations. We laughed together, ministered together, went out on dates, and took trips together. She became an integral part of my life. I enjoyed her personality and her company; it was great being around a young lady who genuinely loved God.

Because she was a servant by nature, she often helped me finish papers for school. If I needed her to run an errand, she would do it. She would either bring me food or cook for me if she thought I was hungry, and she would even do my laundry without my asking. Whatever I needed, her main goal became to satisfy and serve *me*. It was not too difficult to see that I was the primary benefactor in our relationship. For a while, I considered whether she was the one for me, but I couldn't make up my mind. I was undecided and scared and did not want to make a mistake. Quite honestly, our friendship was great and very comfortable just as it was, so I never felt any urgency to make a decision. Deep down, it felt good to be around someone who really cared and had so much affection for me. I also knew that she respected me as a leader in ministry. However, I was too young, too selfish, and too prideful to even consider that her emotional investment in our relationship was far greater than mine.

A year and a half later, after consulting with mentors and spending a lot of time in prayer, I felt the call of God to attend seminary in Texas. A few of my friends, this young lady included, flew with me to Dallas to help me get settled. When they were leaving to head back to California, I pulled her aside and began talking with her. I knew that if I was struggling with the direction of the relationship when we were in the same city, there was no way we would be able to maintain our relationship while we were apart. As a result, I had decided that it would be best for both of us if we just went ahead and ended the relationship.

"I don't think we can have a long-distance relationship," I said.

She responded, "What do you mean? I thought it was just a

matter of time before we got married. We've spent so much time together, and we've gotten to know each other so well." I could see the hurt in her eyes and hear it in her voice. But I continued.

"No," I replied. "I think that God is calling me in another direction, so I'm just going to follow Him." I tried my best to be sensitive and even justified my decision with God's leading. Surely she could understand.

After what seemed like an eternity of awkward silence, she spoke. This young lady, whom I had known to be so gentle, tender, and caring, spoke a very bold statement to me. She looked me square in the eyes and said, "God's got great plans for you, but if you don't fix this issue, it's going to derail you." I couldn't believe what I was hearing. Instead of being overtaken by emotion, she was calling me out! She was basically saying that the way in which I was choosing to deal with our relationship was a warning sign. If I didn't learn how to relate to women in a healthy way, I was going to run into big problems for the rest of my life. I appreciated her concern, but I didn't think much of it beyond that.

I thought that was the end of it; however, several months after she left Dallas I received a phone call from her.

"Conway," she said. "I care about you too much to leave this problem unchecked." I didn't know where she was going with this, but I wanted to hear her out.

"All right; then let's talk about it," I responded.

"No, I don't think you'll listen to me if we talk one-on-one about this issue." Again, I didn't know where her thinking was, but I could not have imagined what came next.

About a week later I got a call from one of the elders at my former church. He said, "Conway, I can't believe what I'm hearing about you from this young lady. We want to fly you back to San Diego and hear your side of the story." I was absolutely shocked and thought, *Has she gotten the elders of my church involved?* Was it that serious? I mean, I knew that I could have handled it better, but this seemed a bit extreme. I couldn't believe they were going to fly me from Texas to California just to have a conversation about a relationship.

I decided to consult some counselors from school and at the church I was currently attending. I asked them if they thought I needed to go back to meet with my former elders. Of the ten people I consulted, nine said the San Diego church was no longer my authority. Therefore I was under no obligation to go back.

But one person said, "You need to return." The Holy Spirit used that individual to convict me. I was being led to go back even though I was not looking forward to it.

My former elders paid the plane fare and flew me back to San Diego. Seemingly in a matter of seconds, I found myself in a room with ten elders from the church. The worship leader, who had been a spiritual mentor for me, the young lady, and her best friend were also in attendance that day. I still wasn't quite sure about what was to transpire, but it was suddenly clear that my charm and charisma weren't going to help me in this situation. It felt like I was about to be interrogated by a congressional committee.

The elders started by asking the young lady to share her story. Over the next hour and fifteen minutes, she told about everything that had taken place in our relationship. Virtually every interaction, conversation, and act of service she afforded me came to the light. Hearing her perspective was startling. She remembered the events in grave detail. Almost every date and every trip we had taken had all been etched in her memory. Although I had never had sex with this young woman, I had gone as far as I could go. In other words, I pushed the envelope regarding physical intimacy.

As she spoke, she shared her heart and deep hurt. By the end of her story, there was not a dry eye in the room, including mine. I was blown away as I listened to her describe our interactions. She bared her soul and talked about how she had expected and anticipated marriage based on the nature of our relationship and my actions toward her. She told everyone in that room how she had trusted me and looked up to me as a boyfriend and a ministry leader, and then she told us all how I had shattered her heart.

With tissues being passed around the room and everybody drying their tears, I was asked if I had anything to say.

"No. Everything she said was true," I managed to respond.

In a word, it was devastating. I had never before understood that my behavior was so irresponsible, and I definitely didn't anticipate how it could adversely affect a woman's heart. The potential impact of what one man's casual actions can do to a woman's heart is astonishing. I had never realized how different the emotions of women are from those of men or how easily they trust us. The weight of what it meant to be a responsible man who loves God came crashing down on me.

The elders of this church are some of the most godly men I know to this day. One of them said to me, "Conway, here's what we need you to do. We'll pay for Christian counseling for you, but we need you to understand that you are responsible for your actions when you approach one of God's precious jewels. We don't want this to happen to another woman, not by your doing. Here's a calling card. Anytime you need to talk, call us at our expense because we care for you; we want to prepare you for what God has in store for you."

When I left that room, my mind was heavy with questions for which I had no answers. How in the world was I supposed to make this right? I cared about this young lady and had never meant to hurt her—but I did. I had wanted us to be able to enjoy a special friendship without the pressure of commitment—but this wasn't possible.

How does a man who's truly in love with God handle this gift called "woman" in such a way that protects her heart and refrains from hurting her in the dating process? Can a man and woman truly just be friends? What are the positive things that a man can do to encourage a woman's emotions in a healthy way?

This experience was the springboard to an extensive personal journey that God was about to take me on so that I could learn the answers and share them with every unmarried person I know. I couldn't even imagine how many men had no clue how their casual behavior could have such a painful impact on women.

Over the remaining chapters, I will share the principles God brought to light during my journey. He showed me how important it is to know myself, know who I am becoming, and how a godly man should interact with women in a way that brings honor to God.

Two

the man
you are becoming

I really enjoy seeing good leadership in action. It was game six of the NBA finals. The Dallas Mavericks won the first two games at home, and everyone thought the series would be a sweep. The Miami Heat, however, rallied to win the next three games in Miami and led the basketball series three games to two, with the last two games to be played in Dallas. Most sportscasters still favored the Mavericks to come back and win the championship, but Pat Riley would have none of it.

Pat Riley, coach of the Miami Heat, told his team that he had packed one suit, one shirt, and one tie. There were two games left, but if Miami won game six, the series would be over and the title would be theirs. Riley saw the victory; he created the vision and the environment so that his team could see it and believe it, as well. He then laid out a strategy to get the team to their destination. Now that's leadership!

Just as Riley led his team with vision, strategy, and a sound model, God is asking Christian men to have a vision for our lives and our relationships. God desires men to develop a strategy that will lead us to our destination—with a willingness to model Christ along the way.

For Pat Riley, that was a one-time event, but God is calling you and me to consistently lead with vision throughout life—with all of its ups and downs.

So what does it take to lead in a godly manner? What does it mean to be a godly man? Since the essence of manhood is to initiate and to lead, you must ask yourself if you are on the way to becoming a leader and a godly man. These are the questions I had to ask myself after what happened in San Diego. Since I wanted to be sure that I would never make that mistake again, I needed some answers.

In the biblical hierarchy of authority, 1 Corinthians 11:3 informs us that God ordained man to be the authority in the relationship between a man and a woman: "But I want you to know that Christ is the head of every man, and the man is the head of a woman, and God is the head of Christ." God created man with an innate sense to operate in that role and to make the first move, to start, and to lead, which implies that a man must be headed in some particular direction. It is therefore inherent in his established role of authority to be a leader.

Just as Christ made the first move and initiated, or led, a relationship with mankind, so it is that man must take the initiative and lead. I know that the verb "lead" can be thought of negatively, especially for contemporary woman. Women today are more in control of their education, careers, and well-being than ever before; consequently, the whole idea of being "led" makes them a little skeptical. This skepticism is supported when, after a cursory glance, they realize some men don't even know why they exist or what journey they are on—let alone how to take someone with them. But, men, if we will step up and really seek to find out who God has called us to be, we can begin to rewrite the many sad stories of failed dating relationships and broken marriages that currently prevail.

In Ephesians 5:25, the Word of God commands husbands to

love their wives as Christ loved the church. Christ loved relentlessly. Moreover, Romans 5:8 reveals that He initiated His love in the midst of rejection. As a single man, how are you preparing yourself to love like this? How will you learn to initiate and lead regardless of potential rejection? What's the first step in taking this kind of serious action?

The first thing we must do to redefine ourselves is to become R.E.A.L. men. Do you want to know what makes a R.E.A.L. man? Here's my take on the idea of being a R.E.A.L. man.

Reject Passivity

First of all, a R.E.A.L. man has vision. If you're a R.E.A.L man, then you know where you are going. In order for a man to know where he's going and move toward that vision, a real man must *reject* passivity. In Genesis 2:15 we read, "The Lord God took the man and placed him in the orchard in Eden to care for and to maintain it." Passivity, or laziness, is not implied anywhere in this passage because God expects men to be active, dynamic, and energetic reflections of Himself. Just as a farmer has to know what vegetable or fruit he wants to grow, then sows the necessary seeds and tends the crop to produce those fruits or vegetables, so a man should know where God wants him to go in life and take the necessary steps to get there. That includes sowing good habits by cultivating and tending the possessions that God gives him; for example, a job, home, physical body, and other resources.

To be successful, every man needs a valid model of what a healthy, godly man looks like. One of the most devastating realities in our culture today is that, for a variety of reasons, many men do not have a viable picture of genuine manhood to use as a frame of reference. In other words, they don't know who they are trying to become. Notice I said *who* they are trying to become, not *what*. Wanting to become a great businessman, an athlete, or a husband still doesn't say *who* you want to be. It simply defines *what* you want to do in life. Having a knowledge of who you are as a person should take precedence over whatever it is that you do as an occupation.

Becoming a healthy and vital man requires you to have a vision for your life, and it means you must be actively pursuing the call of God in your heart. Men, rejecting passivity means we don't just wait for life to happen; we make life happen! We can't allow ourselves to just blend into the scenery. God did not create man to simply exist; we were made to contribute! How will your life make a difference?

Keep Eternity in Mind

Second, a R.E.A.L. man lives for the world that is to come, not for this world. In other words, a R.E.A.L. man lives his life with a view toward *eternity*. Ecclesiastes 3:10–11 (NRSV) states, "I have seen the business that God has given to everyone to be busy with. He has made everything suitable for its time; moreover he has put a sense of past and future into their minds, yet they cannot find out what God has done from the beginning to the end."

All of humanity will forever be restless. The question one must ask is, Why? It is because a man can never be content with simple existence; he must always look deeper for purpose and meaning. According to verse 11, the wisdom of God has "put a sense of the past and future into their minds." This simply means that no experience in this life on earth—no matter how varied, stimulating, or memorable—can provide true contentment because God has placed a restless longing for something eternal in the minds of men.

Taking this concept further, the apostle Paul declares in 2 Corinthians 4:17–18 that this longing is tied to God's intention for man to have an eternal perspective. Therefore, true contentment can only be found in God. As men, we have a responsibility to take seriously the brevity of life and be good stewards here on earth. Living with eternity in our minds means that we live our lives to make God look good, bringing Him glory through the manner in which we choose to live, until He takes us home to heaven. The bottom line is that we must live for what is to come as opposed to simply living for today's gratification.

International students who come to the United States to gain an education are a great example of living with a future goal in mind. When they come to the States, everything they do and buy has to be examined through the eyes of their long-term plan to return home. If they are going to buy a car, get married, or make any major decisions, they have to consider how that will fit into their culture and the goals for their future. They have to be careful of making major purchases because they won't be taking much with them when they return to their home country. They have to travel light and be willing to live in such a way that anyone who encounters them realizes where their long-range focus lies.

What is true of international students attending school in the United States should be true of all men. Just as these students are away from home to accomplish a task, so too is every man of God. We are here on earth to accomplish God's plan for our lives, a plan He has placed within our hearts. Men cannot be so consumed with the accumulation of "things" and becoming successful according to the world's standards that we lose focus on the real reason we're here. In other words, don't burden yourself with temporary things you can't carry back to your eternal home in heaven. If we can't model this mind-set for ourselves, it won't be something we can effectively teach our families.

Be Aware of Strengths and Weaknesses

The third characteristic of a R.E.A.L. man is *awareness*. We must be aware of who we are and how we think. It is important to know how our heritage, life experiences, skills, gifts, and personal temperaments will support us as we interact with women in relationships.

The apostle Paul's claim was that if anyone had the right to brag about his or her earthly status, it was he. He attested to this fact: "I was circumcised on the eighth day, from the people of Israel and the tribe of Benjamin, a Hebrew of Hebrews. I lived according to the law as a Pharisee" (Philippians 3:5). Undeniably, Paul had an elite birthright and lived a high-class life before becoming a Christian.

Why did Paul take the time to say all this? He was leading up to verse 7, where he declared, "But these assets I have come to regard as liabilities because of Christ." The man of God demonstrates a high degree of self-awareness in this passage. He knew himself well enough to know exactly what he was giving up in order to follow Christ. But he also knew his earthly status could be a stumbling block in his ministry if he did not constantly count it all as worthless and "regard it as a liability." Paul's example is a very good one for us to follow. Along with being made ruler over what God gives us and living today in light of eternity, God expects us to be prepared to take ownership of our behavior and our actions, especially in the area of relationships when we are considering marriage.

Being equipped with self-awareness also includes a man's responsibility for the "baggage" he will bring to a relationship. I can't emphasize enough how important it is to have a sense of identity and to know yourself. The experience I shared in chapter 1 opened the door to a profound inner search. That young lady and my elders saw a serious flaw in my character, and if I wanted to grow as a man, I had to dig deeper. Of course, that situation was just the start of a long thread that began to unravel as I discovered the experiences, family background, cultural and spiritual values, and personal beliefs that governed my behavior.

Although we usually don't have a problem identifying them —it is just as important for us to recognize and then utilize our strengths and gifts. As men, our God-given responsibilities include leading courageously, connecting emotionally, loving selflessly, discipling comprehensively, and fighting faithfully against the deceptive influences of the world. We are obligated to try to identify the many facets of ourselves that have the potential to either hinder us or help us in successfully fulfilling these great responsibilities.

Ephesians 5:23 lends support to the truth of why we must take this matter seriously, "Because the husband is the head of the wife as also Christ is the head of the church—he himself being the savior of the body." Men, we cannot be the head of anything or anyone without first being prepared to accept the inherent responsibility that comes with the role of leadership. Are you ready to lead? Are you ready to be the head of your household? Are you ready to disciple a family?

Love Consistently

Are you prepared to *love* someone in a consistent manner? This is the final quality of a R.E.A.L. man. Paul admonished us, "Husbands, love your wives just as Christ loved the church and gave himself for her" (Ephesians. 5:25). One of the greatest qualities about Christ's love for us is its consistency—it never changes. As a result, to love means you must be willing and prepared to give all of yourself for the wife with whom God blesses you. This means loving your potential wife regardless of her actions. Loving her on the good days and on the bad days, on the days when it comes naturally and easily, and on the days when it's a struggle and demands the concerted effort of all your faculties.

Furthermore, having Christ as our model means we must be willing to love our mates until death. Just as we can have confidence in Christ's unchanging and unconditional love for us, your potential mate should have the confidence to believe that you will love her regardless of her behavior, her moods, and her decisions. As believers in Christ, we must learn to love consistently, comprehensively, and completely.

In summary, R.E.A.L men reject passivity, realize that they must keep eternity in mind, are aware of both their strengths and weaknesses, and love consistently. Men, we must be R.E.A.L in all of our relationships, not just with potential mates. Being R.E.A.L. must be a part of our character. If we can't exhibit these qualities with our family, friends, our brothers and sisters in Christ, those who are in authority over us, and coworkers, we cannot expect for these necessary traits to magically appear when we're ready to pursue a woman. Before we can even take the step of praying for God to send us a wife, we must be honest, transparent—and R.E.A.L. —with ourselves and with God who created us.

Having highlighted four important attributes of a godly, R.E.A.L. man, let's talk about how men should interact with women in a healthy way. How can we put action to those attributes? The following are six behaviors from God's Word that will help us better comprehend what it means to be a godly man in the area of maintaining relationships.

1. A godly man does not engage in emotionally based relationships with a woman to whom he has not made a serious commitment to engagement, marriage, and family. If you have a relationship that you use to meet your emotional and/or physical needs as they arise or perhaps a female "friend" who substitutes as a girlfriend whenever you feel like it—you're probably in or headed toward an emotionally based relationship. These are nonfamily relationships in which you play the role of protector, comforter, counselor, or provider, and where either of you would be hurt (even if you wouldn't admit it) if the other entered a similar relationship with someone else. If you cannot see yourself married to a woman with whom you have an emotionally based relationship, then here is the question you must ask yourself: *Is my behavior appropriate for a godly man?*

Genesis 2:24 addresses emotionally based relationships, "That is why a man leaves his father and mother and unites with his wife, and they become a new family." This Scripture underscores the importance of commitment when a man and woman make the decision to come together. Commitment means permanence.

2. A godly man chooses not to lust after a woman (to satisfy himself at her expense). We are exhorted in 2 Timothy 2:22 to "keep away from youthful passions [lusts], and pursue righteousness, faithfulness, love, and peace, in company with others who call on the Lord from a pure heart." This is a decision similar to the one Joseph made when he fled the house of Potiphar in Genesis 39 after Potiphar's wife propositioned him. It's a *choice*, brothers, and you must make the right choice each time you are prompted to do so.

The apostle James wraps it up nicely when he writes, "But each one is tempted when he is lured and enticed by his own desires. Then when desire conceives, it gives birth to sin, and when sin is full grown, it gives birth to death" (James 1:14–15). This means we must try our best to avoid situations that may conceive lust-filled desires in our hearts. It also means when we find ourselves with lust in our hearts we ought to do everything using God's power within us not to act on it.

Look, guys, let's be practical. Sometimes we have to go the extra mile to not take the second look or to make sure our eyes stay on her eyes during conversation. I have some personal boundaries that I maintain, such as not being one-on-one with a woman unless it's absolutely necessary. If it is, I make sure someone else knows where we are and what we're doing and how long it should take. The point is, being visual in nature isn't an excuse for letting lust take up room in our hearts. God knows how He made us, and He still maintains a standard of purity for us.

3. A godly man understands God's design for sex. We read in 1 Corinthians 6:18, "Flee sexual immorality! Every sin a person commits is outside of the body—but the immoral person sins against his own body." Sexual sin involves sinning against one's *own body.* Sex is specifically designed for marriage, and sex outside of marriage can prove detrimental to both the man and the woman. You may think this command is a "given," but you would be surprised how often sex outside of marriage is an issue single Christian men struggle with. Some men are so consumed with their personal struggle that they actually debate the absoluteness of God's Word on this subject.

If you're a man who has engaged in this debate, let's be clear. Sexual purity outside of marriage is not an option! There is no room for interpretation. It is a sin to find sexual fulfillment anywhere else but with your wife. This includes masturbation, all forms of pornography, and any other methods the world or our flesh may invent. As a godly man, you would be wise to remember 1 Corinthians 6:19–20: "Do you not know that your body is the temple of the Holy Spirit who is in you, whom you have from God, and you are not your own? For you were bought at a price. Therefore glorify God with your body."

4. A godly man knows that inappropriate interactions with women can have a lasting negative effect on their view of men and their regard for women. Yes, God is concerned about our day-to-day interactions with women. Therefore we should desire to treat women in a way that honors both them and God. Paul charges Timothy to "speak to . . . younger women as sisters—with complete purity" (1 Timothy 5:1–2). This is a deliberate choice you have to make. Paul reminds us again in Ephesians 4:21–24 when he writes, "If indeed you heard about [Christ] and were taught in him, just as the truth is in Jesus. You were taught with reference to your former way of life to lay aside the old man who is being corrupted in accordance with deceitful desires, to be renewed in the spirit of your mind, and to put on the new man who has been created in God's image—in righteousness and holiness that comes from truth." Paul is basically saying to ditch whatever old habits and tendencies you had that lead to immorality and practice new habits of holiness.

Men, now is the time to put off the former conduct. It's time we move from being *players* to being *protectors*. There is a fine line between being considerate or complimentary and being flirtatious or fishing for compliments. There is a fine line between acting as a gentleman should and treating her like a girlfriend. These lines can sometimes be hard to see, but trust me; they certainly exist in a woman's mind. When in doubt, get advice from the men who hold you accountable and the men who give you counsel. You can even ask your mother, sister, or any female relative. They are usually more than willing to help you draw the line!

5. A godly man views himself as a leader in any relationship and accordingly takes a lead role in the establishment of a godly household. Joshua 24:15 makes the bold declaration, "Choose today whom you will worship. . . . But I and my family will worship the Lord!" Here is yet another reminder of how important it is for us to reject passivity. As men, we set the tone for our homes and our families. However, this is a role you begin to carry out *only* when you are pursuing a woman for a marriage commitment. Herein lies one of the many problems with casual dating. How can you take the lead in a relationship to which you're not committed?

6. A godly man uses God's Word as the ultimate guide for his life. David declares in Psalm 119:105, "Your instructions are a lamp that shows me where to walk, and a light that shines on my path." In fact, this entire psalm is dedicated to the importance of God's Word and His commandments. Today there are so many books on the subject of manhood that we don't know which way to turn. Men sometimes receive mixed messages from preachers too. Who's right? The only way to determine genuine truth is to be led by the light of God's Word. Seeking advice from the pastor with the best of intentions, a very close friend, the wisest counselor, or even this book must be tried and tested by God's unwavering standard. God speaks directly to us through His Word. He gives us guidance and discernment and refreshes us as leaders. Whether or not we realize it, the amount of time we spend in His Word becomes evident in how we conduct our lives.

As we embark on this journey of finding out who God wants us to be and how He wants us to live, it is our duty to seriously commit our lives, bodies, thoughts, dreams, and relationships to Christ. A prayerful and consistent study of God's Word will help you realize the magnitude of who God designed you to be. You can begin to see all of your life—including your relationships—through His eyes.

I can only imagine all of the thoughts swirling through your mind right now. Maybe a personal story can help or at least remind you that you're not alone. On the following pages, one of my mentees shares what he experienced the first time he heard this message on nurturing godly relationships.

o n e
m a n ' s
e x p e r i e n c e

My initial experience *hearing Pastor Conway
teach the message "Engaging the Heart" was
with a group of men who all had a desire to know
what it meant to engage the heart of a woman. I
must admit that my expectations were pretty low
for what I would receive from the session. I expected the time to be a social hour where a
group of men generated more questions than answers, added some spiritual content, and ultimately came away with very little, if anything.*

*Instead, within a short period of time I re-
ceived a new revelation that I still carry with me.
My heart was longing for the answers that my
mind could not exactly comprehend, and I knew
the truth the minute I heard it. Many of the men
in the session that day, whose ages ranged from
eighteen to over forty, began to reflect on past
relationships. In that moment, for the first time,
it all made sense. We had all engaged and captured the hearts of women we had known and,
for the most part, we were clueless to that fact.*

*It was so simple, yet it had eluded me for
years. Who would have ever believed that something as simple as my conversation could engage a woman's heart? In my mind I was just
being friendly with the hope of developing a
friendship but nothing more—well, maybe a little
more—but the rest of the commitment was years
off. I realized that through my conversation and
considerate actions, I could speak to the hearts*

of women with much deeper meaning than I could understand on my own. This revelation has changed me forever.

After I left the session, I had to put aside my previous understanding of how to behave or react toward women. My reality had been shaken up, and I realized that things were a lot more serious than I first perceived. I now had a responsibility to guard the hearts of women and treat them as my sisters. Part of that responsibility meant that I would have to always be on alert when interacting with women.

I now know in a practical way that if a woman is not your wife or engaged to be your wife, then she is your sister and should be treated as such in all purity. I can no longer straddle the fence between friendship and love interest. So until the time when God presents her to me, I do the work that God has given me to serve Him. I work in preparation for what is to come and try to minimize the distractions I encounter as I seek to do His will.

Three

the woman
you are becoming

As a woman, I have discovered that the answers to many of life's questions can be found in one place. You guessed it—the mall! One day I needed a particular item, and I knew the nearby mall would have it. I arrived and found myself standing in the middle of a once-familiar territory feeling quite disoriented. The mall had recently undergone an extensive expansion. It had more than doubled in size, and the number of stores seemed countless. I was there to run a quick errand. I knew what I needed to purchase, and I knew that it was in the mall somewhere, but suddenly I didn't know which store would have it or where that store might be.

I took a chance and started walking in the direction that looked right. I was really lost and only hoped that I was getting closer to my destination and not walking farther away with each step. After passing a few stores, I saw the light. No, it wasn't the store I was looking for. It was better. I had found the mall directory! And of course the first thing I looked for was the little triangle that indicates "You Are Here." Once I realized where I was in relation to my destination, my perspective and methods changed. First, I studied the directory to locate the closest store that would have what I needed. Next, I noted some key landmarks I would need to pass by to get to that store. Then I was off in the right direction, feeling confident, and walking a lot faster than before.

My experience at the mall is similar to our experiences as women. We have destinations that we are trying to reach that may be related to family, career, school, health and fitness, or spiritual growth. Of course, many women have one destination that consumes them more than any other, and that is marriage. The problem is that often we find ourselves being as lost as I was trying to navigate through that mall. We know what we need in general, and we know that only God has it, but we don't know what that looks like in our everyday lives or which direction to go in order to pursue it.

Before you can begin to chart a course for a specific destination, you must know from which direction you're starting. So often we take the approach I initially took. We decide to "take our chances" and start moving in a direction, hoping and praying that we will wind up in the right place. If you walk through the mall long enough, there is always a chance that you'll find the store and items you are looking for. However, striving to be a godly woman doesn't work that way. You can wander for a very long time and still miss the mark. To mature into the woman God has designed you to be, you must first know the woman you are today. One of the big issues in marriages is that people don't realize how much of who they are and how they think shape how they relate to their spouses. Only after you take assessment of where you are in relation to your own baggage, issues, life experiences, and personality can you begin to think about preparing for a relationship, courtship, or marriage.

In the following paragraphs I will outline some foundational biblical characteristics that are critical to fulfilling your role as a woman of God. As you read through them, consider where you are in each category. Identify which area is a particular struggle for you and also determine the areas in which you naturally flourish.

In the beginning, God created the woman to be a helpmate. In essence, He created us to S.E.R.V.E. If the word "serve" makes you cringe—and for many women it will—let me just ask that you stop right now and pray for God to open your mind and make your heart fertile soil for what He has to say.

Ready? Good. Now let's move on.

Support

Woman was originally designed to support and undergird a man who understands his purpose and recognizes his destiny. Genesis 2:18 says, "The Lord God said, 'It is not good for the man to be alone. I will make a companion for him who corresponds to him.'" Her role is not a weak one. On the contrary, it is one of strength and perseverance. However, it is frequently misconstrued as "less than" or "second class." In reality, the woman's role points to her position and not to her value.

If a man is fulfilling his God-given role, he will be working toward a vision, task, or calling that requires a suitable helpmate to support him. When a man is carrying out his God-intended duties as a husband, then the woman's role of supporting him can be realized. Therefore, if she is following a man who needs her help, he must be doing something that he can't do alone. The foundation of that marriage is intact and following divine order. On the other hand, if a man is *not* doing something so big that he needs a woman's help, women tend to get restless. Furthermore, when we get restless, we often step outside of our divinely appointed role of helper and try to take control. Typically the marital relationship becomes strained, and problems naturally arise when the spouses' roles are not in alignment with God's intended plan.

Empower

Second, a woman is called to empower, nurture, and develop those around her. Proverbs 31:12 says, "She brings him good and not evil all the days of her life," and verse 23 states, "Her husband is well-known in the city gate when he sits with the elders of the land." These verses speak about how a woman gives support to her husband—so much so that he draws strength from her and gains a widespread reputation.

Please know that to empower someone does not mean to exercise control over that person. The act of controlling exerts power, but the act of empowerment relinquishes power to another individual. In order for a woman to be one who empowers, she has to give up her desire for credit and recognition. When doing so, she is fulfilling the role of her husband's helper. Her objective is not to overshadow him but rather to promote him. The end result is found in Proverbs 31:31 (KJV), which speaks about the woman who receives blessings from God for her commitment to her marriage union: "Give her of the fruit of her hands; and let her own works praise her in the gates." God is pleased and we are rewarded when we walk in obedience toward Him and follow His plan for our lives.

Relate

We have also been uniquely gifted to relate and connect with others, especially our families. This is the third attribute of a woman who S.E.R.V.E.s. In Proverbs 31:26–28 we read, "She opens her mouth with wisdom, and loving instruction is on her tongue. She watches over the ways of her household, and does not eat the bread of idleness. Her children rise up and call her blessed, her husband also praises her." Not only does this woman relate well to others with wisdom and kindness, she particularly relates well to her family, and they praise her for it.

It is interesting to note that the praises come *after* the verse dealing with her tongue (v. 26). There must be a connection here. Controlling the tongue is a critical area for women to perfect. Unfortunately, the tendency to have sharp tongues has been the cause of many broken relationships and hurt feelings. Depending on how we use it, the tongue can hinder or help us in relating and connecting to others.

Value a Covering

The fourth characteristic of a woman who S.E.R.V.E.s is that she values the covering in her life. Genesis 2:24 talks about a man leaving his mother and father and uniting with his wife. The verse bears repeating here because this principle applies to both men and women. It doesn't necessarily mean that you can't leave your parents' house until you get married. But it does mean that as long as a woman is not married, she shouldn't leave the authority of her mother and/or father. This is because we must *always* be under a covering. God never planned on us living life without a spiritual authority to guide and protect us. As women, we should have a spiritual protector who serves as our covering until we are married. This passage does not indicate a limit on the age of the woman—only that she is unmarried. A woman doesn't outgrow the need for a spiritual covering, and your covering doesn't necessarily have to be older than you or even be related to you.

Having said that, let me encourage you to use wisdom in choosing a spiritual father. If he is not a relative, it is best that he be married and that his wife is someone with whom you have a genuine relationship. The main function of a spiritual father—or spiritual parents—is to provide general godly wisdom as issues in life arise. This is so that you have a sounding board to bring balance to your decisions and choices.

A few years ago, a widow of about sixty decided to remarry. Before she committed to marrying her new love, she made sure that her son and one of her nephews talked with him and assessed his character. She valued them as her spiritual covering. No matter your age, any relationship you are in needs to come under the authority figure in your life. A problem arises because many women have no authority to "leave" and often find that they "unite" with seemingly the first prospect that comes along.

I urge you to value your need for a spiritual covering. If you don't have one, or don't know of any potential candidates, earnestly ask God to provide a covering for you. *A note of caution: Beware of a man who doesn't respect the spiritual father figure or parents in your life. This may clue you in as to how he views authority in general.*

Enhance

Lastly, a woman who S.E.R.V.E.s enhances and impacts the lives of the people around her. Proverbs 31:11–15 says, "The heart of her husband has confidence in her, and he has no lack of gain. She brings him good and not evil all the days of her life. She obtains wool and flax, and she is pleased to work with her hands. She is like the merchant ships; she brings her food from afar. She also gets up while it is still night, and provides food for her household."

Everyone around a woman of virtue is better off because she is in the household. Sometimes our tendency is to focus on enhancing external things. We want to look nice, have a beautiful home, and have attractive and well-groomed children—and these things have their place. However, the most important thing women can enhance is our hearts. When we beautify our spirits, we can greatly influence the lives of everyone around us. As we grow and develop, everyone around us has the opportunity to grow and develop as well. Pause for a moment and consider who you are you becoming. Who is becoming a better person because of your presence in his or her life?

Simply put, being called to S.E.R.V.E. means that we prioritize others over ourselves. Think about the women you admire: mothers, grandmothers, aunts, and sisters. You will discover that they are all givers who consistently prioritize the needs of their families and friends. That is why their influence upon us is so profound. You may be thinking of how much you love and esteem the women in your life and wonder how in the world you'll ever be like them. Often we are more concerned with "being taken advantage of," and we convince ourselves that we can't S.E.R.V.E. others the way our matriarchs and role models have done. But Jesus absolutely prioritized servants when He told the disciples in Matthew 23:11, "The greatest among you will be your servant." He valued and modeled the principle of servanthood, and so should we.

In God's eyes, having the grace to serve is an act of humility and one of the greatest virtues. Jesus' words in Matthew 23:12 echo this truth: "And whoever exalts himself will be humbled, and whoever humbles himself will be exalted." So it follows, that women pursuing God's plan for our lives should operate out of our abilities to: **S**upport, **E**mpower, **R**elate, **V**alue, and **E**nhance. Moreover, this attitude should be consistent in all of our relationships. Are you supportive of your coworkers, your girlfriends, your family members? Do you empower others, or do you have to be in control? Do you respect all of the authority figures God has placed in your life (father, pastor, manager, etc.)? How do you measure up as a woman who is called to S.E.R.V.E?

When you begin to evaluate who you are and where you are in your pursuit of godliness, you can embrace the concept of S.E.R.V.E. and examine yourself in each of those areas. In other words, once you accept the primary functions of a godly woman, you can then find specific principles to practice on a daily basis. Remember, these are principles, and they are not to be interpreted in a restrictive or legalistic sense. The point is not to create more *rules* to follow but to see the fruit that is produced from having a *relationship* with Christ as we purpose in our hearts to be like Him.

The following are eight behaviors from God's Word that we

believe model the actions of a godly woman, specifically in the area of relationships. The goal is to provide you with a guide with which to evaluate yourself and your relationship.

1. A godly woman understands that it is inappropriate to pursue or engage in physical, emotional, or spiritual oneness with a man to whom she is not married. The apostle Paul writes in Ephesians 5:3–4, "But among you there must not be either sexual immorality, impurity of any kind, or greed, as these are not fitting for the saints. Neither should there be vulgar speech, foolish talk, or coarse jesting—all of which are out of character—but rather thanksgiving." Paul says it's about more than just abstaining from sex; to be a true woman of God, it's also about watching what you say and how you behave.

For many women, the struggle in relationships isn't a physical issue; rather, it's of a spiritual and emotional nature. Therefore, to avoid developing spiritual ties, you must conduct yourself appropriately with men whom you consider "friends." So be careful about praying with or sharing other spiritually and emotionally intimate experiences one-on-one with male friends. For example, weddings and funerals can be significantly emotional events, particularly for women. It's best not to casually invite a man to share such events with us. In these instances, the vulnerability of one's heart could be highly exposed, and the potential to be susceptible to the advances of men can be more likely.

We also need to be cautious with whom we express our hopes, dreams, and fears. Women have been designed to "naturally" connect with men, but we must always use wisdom and be on guard about our interactions with the opposite sex. For you it may be a casual relationship with a counselor, friend, coworker, or even a minister. Even if you feel the relationship is strictly platonic or one that is purely on a professional level, a single moment of vulnerability for either of you is all it takes.

We know that the Bible cautions us in 2 Corinthians 6:14 about whom we are to be connected to or yoked with, and there is good reason for such warning. When you least expect it, and with whom you least expect it, those casual interactions can lead to emotional, physical, and spiritual bonds that are meant to be shared only with your husband—or in an intentional courtship that is heading toward marriage. I'm sure that many of you, like me, can attest to experiencing pain from past relationships where emotional bonds were formed either too soon or went too deep, or perhaps both. Those kinds of experiences often leave a woman drained, emotionally wounded, and hindered from being spiritually and emotionally whole.

2. A godly woman dresses modestly so that she does not cause men to stumble, and she trains her thought life not to lust after men. Romans 14:13 underscores this principle: "Therefore we must not pass judgment on one another, but rather determine never to place an obstacle or a trap before a brother or sister." To put it simply, women must be very careful about what they wear. The focus of men's interest is physical by nature. They don't need any help from us in conjuring up physical desire. If this happens to be a struggle for you and you often feel convicted, earnestly pray and ask the Lord to show you how to make the appropriate changes in your dress and lifestyle. God will respond by giving you the grace to help you make the necessary adjustments in your behavior. This is an area where you can expect to mature as you yield to the Holy Spirit. Be confident that He will speak to your heart and give you the wisdom and guidance that you need.

As you pursue the heart of God, you will find that what may have been acceptable in the past is no longer acceptable to you. Growing closer to Christ is supposed to make us question our motives. *Why* do we wear what we wear? What message are we sending? What benefit are we expecting in return? I firmly believe that modesty begins in the heart. If you are genuinely unsure about whether something is appropriate to wear, you also need the practical advice of women you respect who dress modestly. When in doubt, err on the side of being conservative!

And, ladies, let's not forget our duty to lovingly, yet boldly, encourage and challenge younger ladies as to what they wear—not just talk about them as they walk by. I really wish this happened more often among Christian women today. Every woman who dresses immodestly isn't trying to be sensual, sexual, or provocative. Sometimes she just doesn't know better.

3. A godly woman guards her heart by not engaging in premature interactions with men without having a clear direction as to the purpose of the relationship. First Corinthians 7:34 provides insight into this matter: "An unmarried woman or a virgin is concerned about the things of the Lord, to be holy both in body and spirit." Women must be extremely careful with the time they spend with men. Furthermore, that caution shouldn't end once you decide to enter a relationship. In fact, we have to be even more cautious when we are dating.

We women need to be honest with ourselves. There is a reason we are always wondering where a relationship is headed. There is a reason why we often feel frustrated when relationships have no determined path or definition. Don't ignore that desire for direction. We have an innate desire to be led. It is a part of our makeup that is reflected in the divine hierarchy God established in 1 Corinthians 11:3. The relationship between a man and a woman does not suggest that we are inferior to the man because God placed man in authority over us. But as "the head of a woman," that places man in the role of leadership. Consequently, we can find comfort when the men in our lives set clear, specific direction because that protects our hearts and provides security.

It is dangerous to settle for temporary emotional fulfillment when you know that you're in a relationship that is going nowhere. Even if you think you're a tough woman and your life experiences have hardened your emotions, you are still subject to the leading of your heart and can fall prey to its emotional influence. Be bold. Have courage. Get out of that toxic situation! If the man you're dating hasn't set any direction for the relationship, it doesn't mean he's bad or evil. But it could be a good indicator that it's time to evaluate the "health" of the relationship.

You shouldn't set the direction; that's his job. God values you, and you should value yourself. Don't be afraid to hold a man to a standard that doesn't allow for an ambiguous, inconsistent, never-ending type of relationship that carries no commitment to marriage. *A note of caution:* Be careful with men who "over-spiritualize" their delay in making a commitment. When it becomes apparent that they are procrastinating or wavering in making a decision about your relationship, this is a sign that they are unable to make a commitment. Sometimes you need to let them "wait on God" by themselves. Let them call you when they are ready and hope you are still ready and willing.

4. A godly woman enters into a relationship with a commitment to sexual purity before marriage. "Do not be deceived," 1 Corinthians 15:33 admonishes us. "Bad company corrupts good morals." How many times did you tell yourself that the man you were dating was going to change? Sexual purity is hard enough when both the man and the woman totally adhere to God's requirement for it. It's even more difficult when one person in the relationship doesn't fully accept the principle of abstinence. Often, but not always, it is the man who struggles with maintaining purity.

You may think that abstinence is a given, especially when you're dealing with Christians. Don't be deceived. Many single

Christians who love God have yet to surrender this area of their lives to Him. Whatever the case, make sure this is agreed on and understood from the onset of the relationship, set reasonable boundaries, and choose accountability partners who will help you uphold this principle.

5. A godly woman recognizes that God is at the forefront of her life. Her trust is in God and not in her schemes on how to get a man. The apostle Peter wrote in 1 Peter 3:15a, "But set Christ apart as Lord in your hearts." Our minds need to be focused on our one true passion—the Lord and the things that please Him. In order to do this we must be willing to stare loneliness, insecurity, disappointment, and other struggles in the face and declare, "Jesus alone is enough!" Does this sound too spiritual? Well, it's true! A number of women have testified that they weren't even looking to marry when God gave them a husband. A husband is just one thing God can bless a woman with. There are so many other blessings that are realized when we sincerely become consumed with Christ.

6. A godly woman trains herself to have a submissive and servant attitude in all her relationships. Ladies, I can't express how important this is. First Peter 2:18–21 says that your character of service is tested when you're treated unfairly. This is definitely true in marriage. One of the reasons it is so difficult for many women to practice submissiveness in marriage is that they have not taken time to practice it anywhere else. Think of how a selfish, self-centered attitude can cause much damage to a relationship. Have you ever been guilty of this kind of counterproductive behavior?

Try practicing service and submission with girlfriends or family members. It may be something as minor as being agreeable when a group is deciding where to eat. It could be something simple like coming to a friend's aid when it will truly inconvenience you. This is an attitude we should adopt *before* marriage. The truth of the matter is that the behaviors you model as a single woman will be what you take into marriage.

7. *A godly woman recognizes that all men are created in the image of God and therefore should be respected. She rejects disrespecting and complaining about men.* Seeing men through God's eyes is a refreshing perspective that will affect how you relate to them. We need to acknowledge the reality that they all need our support, encouragement, and respect. It is what God requires of us. Further, Ephesians 5:33 commands wives to respect their husbands. Here again, what you practice as a single woman will be the attitude you take into marriage. How do you treat the men you interact with at work, church, or among friends? How are the men in your family treated? Remember, as in all worthwhile endeavors in life—including relationships and marriage—practice makes perfect!

8. *A godly woman understands that the man is the initiator of relationships and she is the responder.* The examples set forth in the lives of Isaac and Rebekah (see Genesis 24:15–67) and in the lives of Hosea and Gomer (see Hosea 1) distinctly show that men are required by God to initiate the relationship, and women are expected to be the responders. However, when the man does initiate, a woman needs to specifically be aware of the precise nature of the relationship he is initiating. Why did he approach you? What is his intention for the relationship? What is his philosophy on relationships? Does he have a vision for himself? Is he interested in protecting your heart? Is his initiation a move of the flesh or the result of a plan covered with prayer? Don't get me wrong. **These aren't the questions you should be asking overtly; however, these are questions that you should**

keep in your mind to observe how he responds in the early stages of your interactions with him. If these important questions remain unanswered for too long, you may be heading into one of those ambiguous relationships we talked about earlier, and the effects of that could be devastating.

Now, what is a woman to think? You've got a lot of information to process. Most of it may already be familiar to you, but now you need to decide what practical changes you may need to make in your behavior and/or your thinking. I know your heart has certain longings for companionship, commitment, and family because God made us that way. But I also know that you have a desire to honor Him with a heart set on righteousness and a lifestyle to match. Following is one woman's story of how God shed light on her unhealthy relationship.

"I Learned the Hard Way"

one
woman's
experience

When I was in the sixth grade, *our school planned a trip to D.C. I went to a private school, where most of the children were affluent and paid for their trip well in advance. That, however, was not my story. Although I had my heart set on this trip, my parents could not afford to pay for it before the final due date. On the final payment date, there was a meeting during lunch in which the teacher explained what would happen on the trip and the things that we needed to bring. I was so excited to be in that meeting I could hardly contain myself.*

Even though my parents hadn't been able to pay until that day, my dad promised me that he would stop by school and bring in the full payment for the trip. So as I sat in the meeting at lunch, I was excited and waiting for my dad to show up. During fifth period, I was still excited and waiting for my dad to come. By the end of seventh period, I was worried but knew in my heart that he would pick me up from school and pay the money then. At 4:00 p.m. my mom picked me up from school and took me home.

I'm over thirty years old now, and I still wonder why my dad never showed up that day. Since that day, I've been subconsciously waiting for someone to "show up," change my circumstances, and take all the anxiety away.

We all know that waiting can be a lonely activity. To deal with the loneliness, I found quick fixes in my male friendships. From the beginning, these friendships were "unhealthy" for me. But until a year ago, I didn't realize that I struggled with having close male friends. I just thought I was the girl who had a lot of friends who were guys. These guys were there to hang out, do the manly household tasks, help with my career, listen to my woes, provide a man's perspective on things, and serve as dates when needed. Most of all my male companions provided a comfort level that made me feel safe when I was with them. This didn't seem to cause any harm at the time. We never crossed any sexual lines, and we always had an understanding that we were "just friends."

That arrangement worked for me and my guy friends until one guy, Mark, captured my heart. Initially, I wasn't drawn to him. He was just this guy I met who was headed to join the ranks of my "friend zone." He wasn't overly attractive, but he was smart, confident, well groomed, charismatic, and good-natured. Somehow Mark never made it to that friend zone, and I ended up dating him for three years. I was convinced he was the person I had been waiting on to show up and take my anxiety away. And he did that—for a while.

I was so captivated by Mark that I quit my job, left my family, and moved in with him.

Never in a million years did I think I would live with a man who was not my husband. I knew I was settling, but I couldn't say no. We had a great relationship. The only problem was that he had a great relationship with someone else, as well. He had met another woman who started out as just a "friend." Mark was everything I wanted and more; but when I found out about his other friend—whom he had been dating since his divorce two years before he met me—I decided it was time to move on.

That relationship only damaged me further. It added to the pain that had been festering since the sixth grade. It took me at least three years to get over it. Then I met Jason. He was the epitome of a tall, dark, and handsome male. Jason was someone I could laugh and talk with. He was a statesman, great cook, and all-around good guy. He allowed me to drop the burden of being all things to all people and let me lean on him for a little while. He became my therapy, and I believed he was making everything "all better." In my mind, Jason was perfect except for two things: 1) he wasn't ready for a relationship, and 2) he had two other female friends such as me.

I was still a little traumatized from my first mistake with Mark, and I couldn't imagine dealing with Jason and his other female friends. Jason and I decided not to date. In my heart, I hoped he would get it together, drop the female friends, and choose only me. It didn't matter that Jason said that he only saw me as a friend or that the intimate part of our relationship was over. It only mattered that he was there whenever I needed him, and that I knew things about him that no one else knew. I felt we had a special friendship, and I didn't want to lose access to him. I decided it was better to be Jason's friend on his terms than to have no contact with him at all. For a second time, I chose to settle for less than what I knew God wanted for me.

What does all this have to do with being a godly woman? My story contains the highlights of two relationships that taught me a valuable lesson about male/female friendships. Allow me to elaborate. I think that men and women can be friends, but I think it requires a lot of honesty and healthy boundaries. I think it's really hard to be friends when two people are attracted to one another and one of them is lying and saying that the other is just a friend in hopes that someday the other person will get a clue. I think many people who call themselves friends aren't honest with their true desires, and that's why this book is so important.

Singles need to be honest with who we are, what we desire, and how our past influences our decisions. We must not allow our desires to make us rush into the dating process too quickly. We need to first make sure we are on the path to becoming healthy individuals, or we'll end up hurting ourselves even more (not to mention those with whom we are in a relationship.) Choosing your life companion is serious, and you should not let the friendship game or past hurts get in the way of establishing healthy relationships.

I've looked for my rescuer in my male friends and in my work. In the midst of it all, I learned *that my "Rescuer" had been there all the time. Now, my desire is no longer that another Mark or Jason would rescue me, but that a man of God is destined to approach me—in God's timing. My prayer is that he would do so with a heart humbled by Christ and an inner strength that is rooted in his confidence in God's calling on his life.*

I was not the only kid who missed out on that sixth-grade field trip. Several other kids did not get to go either. We stayed behind and did mundane work while everyone else went away to have fun. Sometimes being single is a lot like that. You watch your friends "go away" to be married while you remain behind.

As disappointing as that may be at times, I'm still trusting God to send His choice for me. In the meantime, I focus on fostering healthy relationships with females and allowing God to heal me from past hurts so that I will become a restored, emotionally whole vessel that He can use for His work.

Four

who's
your comforter?

Popeye had his spinach, George Burns had his cigars, and Linus had his blanket. What, or who, do you use to help you feel secure or comforted? What do you do when you are lonely, frustrated, confused, angry, stressed, bored, or when you simply want to be loved? Conway loves to play soccer or go for a jog when he needs to relieve a little stress, and I often use a good jog to clear my mind. Sometimes insecurity leads me to the mall to "treat myself." It makes me feel a *little* better for a *little* while. Who or what is your substitute for God during those bad days? What do you do to quench your thirst when life leaves you feeling a little parched? Is God really enough for you? I want to encourage you to let Him bring you full satisfaction in every situation that you encounter.

John 7:37 records, "On the last day of the feast, the greatest day, Jesus stood up and shouted out, 'If anyone is thirsty, let him come to me.'" Jesus was talking to a group of people who by no means should have been thirsty. The context takes place on the *last* day of a *great feast*. These people had been eating and drinking for days. Moreover, the last day of this feast was also traditionally the day of reflection. Jesus wanted to share parting words that they would carry home. So He stood on *an elevation* and shouted a *proclamation*. He definitely wanted their attention.

His invitation held three key words. The first key word is "if," which presents a condition. Jesus knew that some of the people listening to Him were not going to believe or even realize that they were spiritually thirsty. The second key word in Christ's statement is "come." This is an action word that indicates that someone must make a decision to take the initiative. It's critical to consider this because the initiative refers back to the pronoun "him" and represents the thirsty person. The third key word is "Me," which indicates the source to which the thirsty person must go. He must go to the One who can satisfy the need, or quench the thirst. So in verse 37, we see Jesus giving the people an opportunity to: (1) consider their condition and determine that their real thirst has not been satisfied;(2) take action once that thirst is realized; and (3) believe that the solution is found only in Christ.

What are they thirsty for? That's what I asked when I first read this passage. Jesus supplied the answer—they were thirsty for something that never runs out. These people didn't just need a single drink; they needed the renewable resources that only He could offer them. Do you know that because we are all created in God's image, we all have a thirst for something that never runs out? That something, or that *Someone*, is God. If, by faith, you have accepted Christ as your Savior, the grace of God has saved you (Ephesians 2:8).

That means Jesus was talking about you when He said, "Let the one who believes in me drink . . . from within him will flow rivers of living water" (John 7:38). The question is, on a day-to-day basis, are you tapping into your inner source of living water that God has placed inside of you, or are you using substitutes to try and satisfy your thirst? Serious problems can arise if we try to quench this spiritual thirst for something deep, meaningful, and eternal with things that are shallow, meaningless, and temporary, hoping that the cumulative effect will bring genuine satisfaction.

Consider this: Who is your comforter? Is Christ alone enough for you? Are His love and affection for you enough to quench your thirst? If your life is characterized by contentment with who you are and what you're doing, the answer to this question is yes. If you struggle with choosing to be joyful, even during hard times (see James 1:2); or if God is not the first person you run to when you need comfort, the answer for you is probably no. Unfortunately, many of us find ourselves in the "no" category.

When we use our own devices to soothe us when we hurt, it breaks God's heart. God lamented when the Israelites resorted to other means of contentment. He said, "My people have committed a double wrong: they have rejected me, the fountain of life-giving water, and they have dug cisterns for themselves, cracked cisterns which cannot even hold water" (Jeremiah 2:13). They had once again chosen to build idols to worship in place of the true God. God equated those idols to "broken cisterns." Cisterns are built to catch and store rainwater—especially in areas where water is scarce. But a broken or cracked cistern provides little help because the water that it is meant to catch will leak out, and the people who depend on it are left thirsty and still wanting. They will be in the same condition of having no water as they were in before the cistern was built. Actually, it will be an even worse condition because of the time and energy expended only to have nothing to show for it. Even in Jeremiah's time, God tried to show His people that anything they created could never provide the satisfaction and fulfillment they were looking for. They needed to learn to rely on Him and Him alone.

Our list of comforts: shopping, dating, building relationships, working out, spending time with friends, going on vacations, having parties, going to the movies, indulging in food, sleeping, vegging out, drinking alcohol, using drugs, listening to music, and watching the all-powerful "idiot box," television—can all become forms of broken cisterns when we try to use them to hold water that will quench our thirst. Haven't you noticed that after you've done whatever you do to "take your mind off things" that you're still left with the dissatisfaction of having unresolved issues?

Spend some time examining your own situation. What broken cisterns are you relying on—"cisterns" that aren't providing you with any lasting benefit? As a believer, you must acknowledge the sovereignty of God, and believe what He says about His love for you and His plan for your life. Then you can also enjoy the victory and join the apostle Paul in saying, "I am not saying this because I am in need, for I have learned to be content in any circumstance. I have experienced times of need and times of abundance. In any and every circumstance I have learned the secret of contentment, whether I go satisfied or hungry, have plenty or nothing" (Philippians 4:11–12).

You may be asking, "Why should I face the fact that I have a need for comforts? Who cares? What does this have to do with dating or relationships?" To answer these questions, let's first begin with the main reason—God hates it when His children look to temporal things that serve to replace Him. In other words, He dislikes anything that is used as a substitute for Him. He calls it evil, which means it's a sin. Second, it hinders having intimacy with God. In Jeremiah 2, God is angry because His people have built idols to worship in place of Him. We have to be very careful because the things we choose to turn to when we have a need for comfort can also be considered idols in God's eyes. We must know that worship is the expression of our intimacy with God and that intimacy is hampered when we use meaningless replacements for Him. Third, these things will never completely satisfy our thirst. John 7 shows Jesus still addressing the same issue for which God had to chastise His people thousands of years earlier. If our choices for comfort really worked, we would not still be thirsty after we used them. Have you noticed that the things we rely on for comfort rapidly diminish and lose their effect, and the more often we use them, the more we need to revert back to them?

Fourth, we need to face the comforters in our lives because, if we don't, they could lead to unhealthy addictions. One drink doesn't make an alcoholic. One bet doesn't make a compulsive gambler. One desperate phone call to a friend doesn't make a person codependent. We reach the intensity and frequency that define addiction one small step at a time, so we must constantly check our motives for why we do what we do. We must continuously ask ourselves if we're forming unhealthy habits, which lead to life-controlling addictions, even if no one else can see them.

We must deal with this issue of self-examination so that we can determine the role God plays in our lives. The reality is that this is a very important matter, and it's the only way we can passionately pursue God for *who* He is and not *what* He can give us. For many singles, the prospect of marriage is simply another potential "comforter" that they believe will magically bring them the contentment they can truly only find in God. Do you fit into this category? Why would God bless you with one of His sons or daughters as a mate when He knows that you would use that person as a substitute thirst-quencher? We set ourselves and potential mates up for failure when our lack of contentment forces them to meet needs they are incapable of meeting.

The antidote to pursuing comforters and substitutes is finding contentment in God. Most of us live in either one of two "tents"—contentment or discontentment. The question is, in which tent do you reside? Many singles find themselves utterly discontent with the fact that they are unmarried. Furthermore, one of the primary reasons marriages fail is the inability of spouses to be content in the situations that God allows in their lives. If you're not sure which tent you live in, ask yourself *why* you want to be married. If you desire marriage or even a dating relationship as a cure for something else, such as loneliness, or to fulfill the need for love, friendship, or companionship—this is an unhealthy perspective. Think about how you would respond if you were somehow to find out that you will never be married. What if it turned out that you would be married for less than five years before your spouse became seriously ill or died? If these thoughts make you cringe, without realizing it, you may be using the idea of marriage as a form of finding contentment. If so, this could actually be the equivalent of a broken cistern in your life because marriage alone cannot satisfy your thirst for God.

We all know people who are never satisfied. The first sin committed by mankind was rooted in discontentment. Adam and Eve weren't satisfied with God's provision for them in the garden of Eden. They had everything they could possibly need, but they wanted the one thing they couldn't have. It became their focus and ultimately their downfall. Their lack of contentment forced them to miss out on the richest blessing—an intimate relationship and everlasting communion with God.

The Devil uses the same strategy against singles today that he used against Adam and Eve in the beginning. He simply distracts them and gets them to focus on the thing they do not have, that is, a mate. The Enemy then plants seeds of discontentment, which in the end will cause them to miss out on the many things they do have. Things such as flexibility, freedom, unrestricted resources, and availability for ministry are just a few of the things God lovingly gives singles.

What can you do to avoid falling into the traps of your own flesh, the Devil, and the world? You should make it your goal to cultivate the contentment and joy that Paul encouraged the Philippians to have. In doing so, you will soon discover that you will only find true comfort in God. The apostle Paul describes God as "the God of all comfort" (2 Corinthians 1:3 KJV). Nothing or no one can be a match for the comfort God provides and the contentment we find in Him.

What can we learn from God's Word on how to cultivate contentment? To increase your desire to find contentment in Him, study the Scriptures referenced below and ask God to open the eyes of your understanding so that you can discover His plans for you to achieve excellence in your life.

1. Believe that God knows you best (Psalm 139:1–12). One of the most comforting thoughts is found in knowing that God is intimately acquainted with all of our ways. To recognize that God knows our thoughts and our every move provides an overwhelming sense of security. This knowledge allows us to be *completely* honest with God. We can bare our feelings and bring *all* of our care and concerns to Him. Not only will He listen, God has the power to help us turn situations around for good. No one else can know us and accept us the way God does.

2. Trust that God has a plan for your life and that it is in your best interest (Jeremiah 29:11). Every time we doubt our life circumstances, we ultimately doubt God. Notice the word *circumstances* is quite different from the word *consequences*. *Consequences* are the results of our own sinful actions and poor decisions. But even so, God does not allow the consequences of our behavior to utterly destroy us. On the other hand, our *circumstances* are the things we usually don't have control over. We need to trust God when we experience broken relationships, job layoffs, illness, and the loss of loved ones. When no one seems to be interested in our lives, when we don't feel attractive, when we aren't as successful as we want to be, and when the dream of fulfillment we seek seems to keep getting delayed, we must believe and cling to God's promise in Jeremiah 29:11 and trust that He has a plan for our success and not our failure.

3. Praise God for who He is and who He made you to be (Psalm 139:13–17). In Psalm 139 David is thankful because God has made him in a great and marvelous way. It brought David much joy and gratefulness simply to reflect that God had uniquely crafted him. If you genuinely believe that your Creator took superb care in forming you, then you have just accepted the utmost compliment and the greatest affirmation. When you focus on God's Word about you and what He has done in creating you, the diluted affirmations that the world, the Enemy, and your flesh offer will dwarf in significance.

4. Know that you are growing and making progress (Philippians 1:6; 2:13). So often we look at our lives and beg God to help us make a little bit of progress or show some sign of growth. One of the most frustrating things is feeling as if you're expending energy without results. But Philippians 1:6 assures us that God is still working on us from *within*, so we don't have to chase after the world's icons of success. The truth is, whether you possess the latest car, newest home, or trendiest wardrobe, God is still doing a "good work" in you. It is a matter of faith to know that God will empower and encourage you along the way as you press on in your journey with Him. As you extend your faith, your confidence will grow and give you the assurance that He will finish the work He has begun.

5. Ask and then allow God to remove from your heart wrong motives that lead you to seek substitutes for Him (Psalm 139:23–24). After David spent time reflecting on the amazing intimacy he had with God and how well God knew him, he then asked God to search his heart. David wanted to be sure that any wrong thoughts were removed so that he could fully walk in righteousness. Similarly, we have to surrender our hearts to God and ask Him to show us where we need to be corrected.

"Anxious thoughts," as the psalmist calls them (v. 23 NIV), become fertile ground for discontentment and are often at the root of the deceptions that lead us to seek out substitutes for God. David knew the importance of having a pure heart before God. If our hearts are not in alignment with God and seeking His will for us, we can easily be deceived and led astray from Him.

6. Think on things that are right (Philippians 4:8; Romans 8:6–7). The apostle Paul says a mind set on things of the flesh leads to death, but a mind set on the Spirit contains life and peace. To be pleasing to God, we know that our minds must be subject to the things of Christ (2 Corinthians 10:5). Therefore, we must meditate on things that are true, pure, lovely, excellent, honorable, right, of good repute, and praiseworthy. Whew! That doesn't leave room for much else—and that, my friend, is the point.

7. Hang around contented people who can encourage you (Job 6:14; Proverbs 17:17). Biblical wisdom contends that a man's friends should bring kindness when he in is despair; in fact, friends should love at all times. Friends who love relentlessly will provide godly support and encouragement when we face moments of weakness. We need people with whom we have authentic relationships to help us when we are too vulnerable to make sound judgments and decisions. If you want to move from discontentment to contentment, it is vitally important to have friends who can help you make the journey.

When we begin to choose joy and contentment instead of allowing our feelings and circumstances to dictate our behavior, we start to see God in a brand-new way. This new perspective not only draws us closer to Him, but it also helps us to have realistic expectations for everything else in our lives, including dating relationships that lead to healthy marriages.

Five

experiencing healthy relationships

We live in a world where physical and emotional promiscuity is very prevalent. Guys engage in unhealthy, codependent relationships with women. Some women strive to hold on to men who do not desire a commitment. The culture of our day encourages individuals to simply date to marry rather than marry to date. People want the benefits of marriage without the responsibility and the commitment that is inherent in the marriage union. They want to enjoy the companionship, comfort, protection, and even financial benefits without entering the covenant that God has established for marriage.

Often through relationships that can only be defined as unhealthy, women are searching for any support and protection that men can offer, and men are in need of the nurturing environment women are capable of providing. All of this toxic activity is being carried on in the name of dating. And as a result, many people find themselves emotionally connected during the dating process, and subsequently they become quite devastated when the relationship ends. This is a dangerous situation in which to be involved, because an emotional connectivity of this nature was designed for marriage only and not for a dating relationship. But how do we solve this problem?

The disintegration of the institution of marriage has led to our culture losing one of its most powerful images—relationships between men and women thriving in a healthy environment. The result instead is that we have models of unhealthy, codependent, abusive, and self-centered relationships. With poor family models, our culture then decides what is right and what is wrong—not based on God's Word but on what feels good and what satisfies oneself. What impact does this have on today's singles?

The ill effects of society definitely influenced the relationship described in chapter 1 where I prioritized my feelings and my needs over the young lady's. In the final phase of that learning experience, I identified seven biblical truths that brought me closer to seeing relationships and marriage the way God designed them.

1. Genesis 2:15–18 indicates that men are to be the initiators and women are to be the responders when it comes to establishing personal contact with each another. In keeping with this divine order, it is critically important that men understand their God-given role as initiators. The truth is, the choice Adam made to follow Eve's initiative and eat the forbidden fruit put all of mankind under a curse. The results of their disobedience to God's command reversed the roles of man and woman. Moreover, we are still suffering from the consequences of that sinful act to this day.

Out of necessity, many women try to carry the burden of leadership when men willingly take on a passive role. Even the way families are portrayed on television and in movies reinforce this role reversal. We do not often see family images in which the husband is noticeably the leader and the wife respects him as such. If we are to turn the tide on unhealthy relationships, we must first reverse this pattern. Men must accept their God-given role to initiate, direct, and lead; and women must accept their God-given role to support, enhance, and connect with their spouses as God leads their way.

2. I also realized that I needed to focus intentionally on developing healthy male friendships. But, in fact, the reality for me is that it is simply easier to have opposite-sex "best friends," because there can be a mystery and chemistry that surrounds such a relationship. Both men and women naturally form bonds with the opposite sex, and their friendships in many cases prove to be gratifying and enduring.

On the other hand, I have found that having authentic friendships within the same sex can be difficult and rare. In order for same-sex friendships to last, it takes old-fashioned hard work, consistency, and most of all, a demonstration of the fruit of the Spirit. By that I mean that the natural chemistry between men and women often masks character flaws. But for two women or two men to maintain an authentic friendship requires the kind of spiritual work that genuinely produces the fruit of the Spirit. For example, a woman tends to be more forgiving when her male friend forgets to call her on an important matter, but she may hold a grudge against a female friend for displaying the same level of insensitivity. She must learn how to show kindness and love in order to maintain her relationship with her female friend. Another example is when a man overlooks his female friend's constant tardiness but will not tolerate the same behavior from one of his male friends. He has to practice patience to maintain a healthy relationship with his male friend.

Learning to have meaningful, long-term friendships with people of the same sex also forces you to deal with a lot of issues that are common to both parties. It is often said that men can't trust other men because of their pride, and women can't trust other women because they tend to be emotional. I believe this is why many men only have female friends and many women only have male friends.

But many problems occur in building relationships simply because people have difficulty relating to one another when they judge based on superficial traits such as attractiveness or talent and not on character and selflessness. To foster personal development and strengthen relationships, one solution for members of the same sex is to have accountability partners. These faithful friends can help them become more aware of who they are and of the internal issues they need to work on and develop. For example, when men have spiritual brothers who are their best friends and who hold them accountable, it forces them to be men of integrity and exhibit the fruit of the Spirit in their relationships. Similarly, when women have close girlfriends who serve as their accountability partners and in whom they can confide without fear of that confidence being broken, these friends help them to be women of integrity and spiritual maturity.

3. During the process of self-examination, I was reminded of the principle of selflessness. It is a crucial factor to the success of a healthy relationship (see Philippians 2:1–5). People are driven by many forces today. Some are driven by fear and some by pride. Still others are driven by the pursuit of success. But seldom is the motivation to exalt or lift up another person. People tend to be more concerned with helping themselves than with helping someone else.

As Christians are called to consistently consider others above ourselves. In James 4:1–3, we learn that the reason for poor relationships and conflicts is our flawed motives and self-centeredness. Therefore, in order to lead the turnaround from unhealthy to healthy relationships, we must cultivate the habit of selflessness and genuinely prioritize others above ourselves. In the process of change, God will be pleased with our behavior as we model Christ and adhere to the Word of God: "Instead of being motivated by selfish ambition or vanity, each of you should, in humility, be moved to treat one another as more important than yourself. Each of you should be concerned not only about your own interests, but about the interests of others as well" (Philippians 2:3–4).

4. Living by faith was another principle God reinforced in me. It is a natural tendency to live by sight and not by faith when looking for a mate or pursuing a relationship. We crave instant gratification, which means that we primarily trust what we can see and touch. For this reason, many men argue that they have to "test" a woman for a couple of years before they can commit, or many women contend that they have to observe the man in all the seasons before they can make any kind of commitment. The problem with this type of thinking is that it's all about sight, not about faith. But the Bible teaches us in Hebrews 11:6 that without faith it is impossible to please God.

When it's time to select a mate, most of you probably have a "list." That list is supposed to capture all of the "must haves" regarding the characteristics of a potential spouse. Anytime you meet someone who has qualities from your list, you begin to wonder if he or she might be "the one." That type of thinking seems to leave God out of the equation. Anything can happen at anytime to change the ideal scenario. That is why I believe we don't have to date for a year or two to see how the relationship is going to work, nor do we have to know everything about someone to make up our minds. A major part of the decision is the faith factor. We must do all the observation and evaluation, refrain from getting the emotions involved or engaging the heart, and *then* we must trust God to move us forward by faith and with wisdom.

5. Proverbs 27:6 tells us, "Faithful are the wounds of a friend, but the kisses of an enemy are excessive." This simply means that a real friend will tell you what you need to hear—not just what you want to hear. This is accountability at its best, and I learned firsthand how important it is. If I had allowed more people to hold me accountable from the beginning, they would have questioned the intent and direction of the relationship I described in chapter 1. A strong support/accountability system is paramount for healthy relationships.

True accountability is rare in our culture because we often seek to be the master of our destiny, and we often lack the courage to speak truth into one another's lives. But true life transformation really happens best when we have a small group of friends who love God and share our values for righteousness, those who will challenge and encourage us when the major events of life occur. To truly enjoy the benefits of accountability relationships, we must be willing to be vulnerable and open. If we are going to reverse the trend toward developing poor relationships, we must connect with a group of like-minded individuals who will hold us accountable to a God-ordained value system and to living godly in a warped culture.

6. Contentment should be reemphasized here as another foundational element of having a balanced relationship that pleases God. The world is suffering from chronic discontentment, but healthy relationships are cultivated in the soil of contentment. If you are single and unsatisfied, chances are you will be married and unsatisfied. Satisfaction comes from our relationship with God, not from our marital status—or from any other life circumstance. In Philippians 4:11 the apostle Paul asserts, "I have learned to be content in any circumstance." This means that God alone was enough for Paul. For him, it wasn't God plus something else. If you purpose in your heart to adopt Paul's thinking, you will begin to see your relationship—or future relationship—in a much more balanced light with more realistic expectations.

7. Finally, our love for God must be preeminent over all else. Our love for God should be the supreme love Jesus references in Matthew 22:37. If we just exist, we will be caught up in loving the world and all of its messages more than we love God. The world around us is rapidly going downstream, and God has called us to go against the current and swim upstream. The world's lure is so appealing that most of us are simply following its direction without even knowing it. Choosing to love God more than the world is a matter of consumption. What are you consumed with? Work? Friends? Status? Appearance? If you're not sure, take a look at your bank statement. Where do you spend your money? Take a look at your planner. Where do you spend your time? When God is our first love, He has first dibs on our resources, time, body, and mind.

If you begin to look for ways to apply these truths to your life, you can ignite a revolution of developing strong, loving, and healthy relationships with an approach based on biblical values. But what about the subtle issues that threaten to disrupt the cultivation of healthy relationships? How do men and women relate to each other in a God-honoring way? How does a man treat a woman like a sister with all purity? How can men and women guard their hearts? How can singles avoid the hurt and the pain that so often plague Christians in relationships?

The Bible often uses relationships among family members to describe how the body of Christ ought to relate to one another. Paul presents this principle in 1 Timothy 5:1–2 where he writes, "Do not address an older man harshly but appeal to him as a father. Speak to younger men as brothers, older women as mothers, and younger women as sisters—with complete purity." Brothers, from a relational standpoint, we are to treat women with whom we come in contact as we would our very own sisters. Would you romance your sister? Would you give her gifts that entice her to invest her emotions in you without a commitment? Would you caress and kiss your sister? Would you have sexual relations with her? Undoubtedly not—to do so would go against God's Word in Leviticus 18:6–9, "No man is to approach any close relative to have sexual intercourse with her. . . ." Verse 9 of the King James Version reads, "The nakedness of thy sister . . . thou shall not uncover."

Although I did not have sexual relations with the young woman that I discussed in the first chapter, I did not treat her with the purity I would treat my own sister because I failed to comprehend the magnitude of what it meant to protect her heart. Now that's a powerful principle. How does a man protect a woman's heart and avoid hurting her in the dating process?

Psalm 141:3 says, "O Lord, place a guard on my mouth! Protect the opening of my lips!" Even though it is helpful to think of each other as siblings, that doesn't imply that we share everything we would share with a brother or sister. Does that make sense? Some dating couples talk so freely about marriage, children, and having the ideal home that they begin to assume commitment exists when there is none. Once that line has been crossed and the relationship ends, the woman often feels cheated as she looks back, and the man usually feels misunderstood.

Brothers, as the initiators, you have a responsibility to guard a woman's heart at all times during your interactions with her. Sisters, you have a responsibility to "guard your heart with all vigilance, for from it are the sources of life" (Proverbs 4:23). The task of guarding your heart means to keep from turning your emotions over to someone who might be found untrustworthy. Whether the commitment is within the context of the accountability groups mentioned earlier, or with a marriage partner, your heart should be available only to people who genuinely care about you and seek your best interest.

Another term for guarding the heart is emotional abstinence. In her book *The Dating Trap,* Martha Ruppert suggests that emotional abstinence means we do not allow our emotions to be manipulated, nor do we use our emotions to manipulate others. It means we do not give our hearts away to any number of people as we await a wedding day. Christians aren't supposed to rely on emotions as a compass to guide our lives. Yet we have the misconception that if we are guarded about our emotions, then we are not loving, and the chance at love may pass us by. Of course romance and love are not wrong. But neither are they supposed to be recreational activities. Being emotionally vulnerable is not something we practice so we will be ready for marriage. Vulnerability is something we protect so we will be prepared to give freely in marriage.

In order to practice emotional abstinence, you can use some of these practical precautions:

1. Be selective about what areas of your life you expose to others (family, church, special occasions, etc.). Some areas of our lives should require from others a level of commitment before we grant access to them. Sharing very personal experiences too early with others can create a premature sense of intimacy in a relationship. As soon as you feel betrayed, sharing these experiences could be the first thing you'll regret.

2. Be discerning about sharing intimate emotions. Your deepest fears, intimate prayer requests, dreams, and insecurities are treasures to be revealed with caution and only to people who are choosing to journey with you over the long haul.

3. When relating to men, take what they say at face value. Sometimes a man may say something only because he knows a woman wants to hear it. But men generally mean what they say. Ladies, if you are dating a man and he says, "I'm not ready for commitment," that *literally* means he's not ready for commitment. If you choose to proceed with the relationship, hoping to change his mind, you could be sorely disappointed when it's all said and done. There's nothing you can do to change his mind, but there is a lot you can do to control your own mind and actions. Use wisdom and wise counsel to help manage the tendency to take things further in your mind than they may be in reality. For example, *don't visualize the wedding day on the first date!*

4. When relating to women, read between the lines. This doesn't mean that you should make up things that don't exist. It just means that if a woman says something, her behavior should be consistent with what she says. If it's not, you may need to challenge her on what she expressed verbally. Sometimes a woman might say things that she thinks a man wants to hear, but in reality it may be a misrepresentation of how she actually feels. For example, *if she says she only likes you as a friend but questions where you go and who you spend your time with, you need to read between the lines!*

Joshua Harris, the author of the books *I Kissed Dating Goodbye, Boy Meets Girl,* and *Sex Is Not the Problem (Lust Is),* wrote, "The job of guarding our hearts is a big responsibility. It takes place in the secret places of devotion. In honest prayer and meditation on God's Word, we scrape the film of infatuation, lust, and self-pity from our hearts. . . . The work is never done. We must police our hearts with faithful, silent regularity."

Remember, too, we help guard the hearts of others by not luring them into trusting us with their minds, wills, and emotions before we are committed to their welfare.

AN ILLUSTRATION

engaging the heart

one
couple's
experience

I was a content single female who was truly enjoying what God was doing in my life. I was traveling the country as a consultant and loved all the freedom and independence that I had. My singleness was a gift, and I was thoroughly enjoying it—I wasn't looking for a boyfriend. I believed that God would one day bless me with a mate (my plan was for that to happen in at least four years), but I made a decision to trust and obey the Lord even if He never gave me a husband.

It was during this time that I sat down and talked with Conway for the first time. I shared my testimony, discussed ways I could serve in the singles ministry, and then somehow started talking about relationships. He asked me about my "dating requirements list" and challenged me to revise it. You know the list, the one that almost every girl has that describes, in detail, all the characteristics a man must have in order to even have a chance in dating her. I, of course, had "must be a Christian" as the number one requirement, and then other stipulations regarding annual salary, level of education, height, and ability to speak proper English. Conway's

challenge to me was to make all the "requirements" biblical and to make sure that they would
lead to a successful marriage.

He even challenged me to narrow my list
(which was well over ten requirements) down to
three! I told him that would be impossible. But
after a lot of complaining, I revised my list. I
eventually got it down to fulfilling the Great
Commandment and the Great Commission.
"Jesus said to him, 'Love the Lord your God with
all your heart, with all your soul, and with all
your mind. This is the first and greatest commandment.' The second is like it: 'Love your
neighbor as yourself'" (Matthew 22:37–39) and
"Therefore go and make disciples of all nations"
(Matthew 28:19). I then waited patiently to see
what the Lord would do.

In the summer of 2004, I was introduced to
Mr. T. through mutual friends. I learned about his
involvement in the ministry at the University of
North Texas and became a big fan of his music. I
was truly impressed with his heart of service and
thought that he was an awesome man of God,
concluding that he'd make someone a good
husband one day. After really only having known
Mr. T. as a friend of a friend, a more relevant
friendship emerged between us in July 2005. I
was in Golden, Missouri, serving as a volunteer
counselor at Kids Across America, and he was
there as well for a Fourth of July concert. I found
out later that he noticed my service and saw certain qualities in me that sparked his interest. Before approaching me, he asked people at camp
who knew me well—our mutual friends, other

counselors, and even the camp director—about my character and what kind of person I was.

After getting back a "positive report," he began his pursuit. He called me at the end of July with the hopes of getting to know me better. I was excited that this guy was calling me, but wouldn't let myself draw conclusions that weren't based on reality. I decided to think on those things that were true, noble, and trustworthy (see Philippians 4:8), and what was true for me was that we were nothing more than friends. We got to know each other better through talking on the phone and hanging out together at the mall. I told my girlfriends and accountability partners about my new friend, and they encouraged me to make sure my motivations for allowing him to engage me in conversation were pure and that we were being wise with the amount of time we talked on the phone. I listened. Having made mistakes in the past relative to pursuing a man, I was careful to not pursue him. I chose to guard my heart by allowing him to initiate conversations and times to hang out. He was going to have to pursue me.

After a few weeks of being friends, he clarified his intentions by saying that he was interested in pursuing a relationship with me. It would be a relationship that would hopefully lead to a courtship and end in marriage. He shared his feelings for me and told me about the qualities he had observed in me over time. It was then my turn to observe Mr. T. more so that I could make the decision of whether or not I truly wanted to engage in a courtship with him. Having already observed in him all the qualities on *my revised "dating requirements list," I asked people in his life about his character. I also asked him to meet with Conway, my spiritual covering, so that Conway could check him out for me and validate his character. For a month I watched him in service and observed the five timeless traits of faithfulness, awareness, initiative, teachability, and humility before God in Mr. T.; and in September 2005 we decided to enter into a courtship, praying that it would end in marriage.*

During our courtship, we each individually met with Conway, his pastor, and other married couples who served as mentor couples. We read a book together called Define the Relationship, which offers advice to guide couples through dating. With biblical teaching, it helps couples to work through their dating relationships successfully by either deciding to enter into an engagement or to end the relationship. This book guided us through developing physical and emotional boundaries, resolving conflict, discussing past sins, and periodically evaluating our relationship to ensure that we both were still on the same track to marriage.

As we continued to grow as a couple, we faced many struggles: finances, jobs, the desire for children, and familial conflict. Having lived as "Miss Independent" for so long, I struggled with the idea of submission and the roles that the Lord has given men and women in marriage. The root issues of many of our arguments were selfishness, impatience, lack of confidence in the Lord's sovereignty, pride, and the lack of willingness to deny self.

During our relationship, we were diligent in prayer and Bible study. We also sought godly counsel from those around us so that we would be able to discern God's pleasing and perfect will for our lives as described in Romans 12:2. Many times we wanted to give up; I know I wanted to walk away on many different occasions because things weren't going as I expected. Mr. T. and I didn't seem to be compatible, and I was miserable.

Initially, I resented Conway for asking me to change my "dating requirements list." I later learned that we couldn't cling to compatibility with each other—we had to cling to Christ. In March 2006, after lots of joy, fun, trials, tests, fasting, and prayer, we made the decision to join together in marriage. We were finally convinced that we could together—as one—glorify the Lord and do more for His kingdom than we could do separately as singles. We weren't officially engaged until May 2006, but we committed ourselves in March to prepare for a wedding—and more important, a lasting marriage.

got f.a.i.t.h.?

What's next? This might be what you're asking as you continue to progress on the journey of becoming who God has called you to be. Prayerfully you are grasping the principles of what it means to be a godly man or woman and recognizing the importance of guarding your heart. But as a single, you may still be wondering how you will find the man or woman whom God has called to be your lifetime mate.

We have already established that the course of action for recognizing a future mate is fulfilled through the dating process. That is why dating activities must be taken seriously. To avoid some obvious pitfalls, it is important to be aware of the problem with some common approaches to dating. Our culture tells us to do what feels right, judge the book by its cover, and test the "merchandise" before we buy. Unfortunately, none of these approaches include the counsel and guidance that only God can provide a man and woman who are dating and contemplating marriage. Therefore, many people spend more time planning the wedding ceremony than planning for the marriage to succeed. The result of this careless approach then becomes: if it doesn't work out, we can always justify getting a divorce by claiming "irreconcilable differences."

What is evident in our culture is that the current dating approaches are leading to a divorce rate of over 50 percent. In order to avoid this devastating result, we must examine what happens *before* we enter marriage, not simply why we stop liking each other *after* marriage.

There are many questions facing singles who are in the dating arena today. Here are a few:

❖ *How and where will I find my potential mate?*

❖ *How many of my preferences should I hold out for?*

❖ *Is the person I am dating a phony or the real deal?*

❖ *Is the person I am interested in just performing? Will everything change after the wedding?*

❖ *If he or she is having sex with me now and violating God's guidelines, what proof do I have that he or she will be faithful after we get married?*

❖ *Why does it seem as if everyone I date is flaky (noncommittal) and does not share the same values I do?*

❖ *How long should a dating relationship last before I make a decision for marriage?*

❖ *How can I look at a person's current life and determine if he or she will make a good mate?*

❖ *What do I do if I don't have Christian parents or a Christian model to follow?*

Because most dating strategies don't provide objective guidelines for couples to adhere to, both men and women find themselves somewhat perplexed. They are searching for answers to the questions above, and rightly so, because having God's perspective on the subject of dating is *extremely crucial* in their decision-making process for finding the right mate. Without knowing how to go about dating in the proper way, they are ill-equipped and mostly unaware of the best way to approach this very serious period in their lives. With the lack of a comprehensive plan, such people don't like the results they receive because they overemphasize the issue of finding someone who is compatible. However, this is only a part of the entire journey of finding the right mate. We cannot emphasize enough how it is paramount that you do *not* leave God out of the whole dating equation if your desire is to find the right mate with whom you will live a long and fruitful life together.

The following processes, one for men and one for women, are designed to help singles customize an approach that will assist them in avoiding the games people play in dating and allow them to apply a general plan to help them think through the dating/courting process from a divine perspective.

For Men Only

WHO is this for?
Men

WHAT is their role?
Pursuers *(men are to initiate the relationship)*

WHAT should they do?
1. Be Under a "Covering" (have a mentor/spiritual father). In the ideal situation, singles should have parents who provide wisdom and direction. If this is not the case, then you should seek wisdom and direction from a mentor and a spiritual father. This should be someone who knows you well and has your best interests at heart.

2. Identify Timeless Traits. This is the "list." What are you looking for in a mate? Before you meet someone, you should identify not just your *preferences* but *principles* that the Bible supports. (We will address this topic in the second half of this chapter.)

3. Observe Your Potential Mate. Without her knowing that you are observing her, look to see if the woman of your interest possesses the timeless traits you've identified. Ask the people in her sphere of influence questions related to her character. Include as many of her friends as possible, casual acquaintances, people she may not be so friendly with, family members, ministry leaders, and associates. You may be surprised what you can learn from people with whom she interacts. The idea is to gather information about her character, including how she interacts with people she doesn't necessary get along with. It's important not to discard or dismiss any negative sentiments you may receive from people about her. If you do encounter people with whom she has had difficulty relating, try to find out why and under what circumstances. We're not saying to take their opinions as law, but do consider them within the context of your overall observations and what you are learning about her character.

If you wait to try to observe these traits after you formally meet her, then you will have a hard time being objective. This could possibly result in her being hurt if you decide you are not interested and don't want to pursue a relationship with her. You may also run the risk of her altering her behavior in ways that may attract your attention but that do not reflect her genuine personality.

4. Make Contact. Approach the woman you've observed with a plan in mind that has been inspired by your earnest prayers that God has given you a "green light." Keep in mind that she has not yet had the opportunity to observe you. Also be careful to avoid imposing yourself on her and behaving in ways that can be construed as stalking. If she doesn't want to meet with you, move on. You certainly don't want to force a relationship.

5. Engage Her Heart. The more you interact with and speak to her, you must recognize that it is very likely that her heart is being engaged or emotionally invested—even if she doesn't admit it. Even so, the interaction can be done in a considerate and respectful way. As the man, you now have the responsibility to continue to treat her like a sister until she accepts the invitation to become friends, which could lead to courtship. Think of it this way—if the relationship does not lead to marriage, she should be better off for having known you, not regretting the day she met you.

6. Enter a Courtship with an Agreed-Upon, Specific Timeline. After you've secured permission from her spiritual covering and there is an agreement to continue toward courtship, then you must set clear directions. She should never have to guess or wonder about your intentions. At this point, setting a general time frame for the relationship is also necessary to avoid any misunderstanding about the seriousness of your intentions. This means that both people agree that marriage is the destination. The wedding date can be set because the proposal could happen at any time. If it hasn't already been done, ideally a mentor couple is identified by this time to help you both navigate your way.

7. Get Engaged. Obviously, this is when you ask the big question. Guys, when you pose the question you should already be certain of the answer, because there has been continuous communication throughout the process. During this stage, you and your fiancée may choose to make more permanent decisions regarding career, finances, family, and other important decisions to consider. But continue to be careful. Until you are married, you are still separate in God's eyes. A highly recommended practice is to seek out premarital counseling at this time.

8. Get Married. Now the *real* work begins!

9. Continue to Meet with Your Mentor Couple. Regular meetings should be set up with your mentor couple. If and when problems arise, either individual should feel free to contact the mentor couple for help in resolving the issue in a godly way.

For Women Only

WHO is this for?
Women

WHAT is their role?
Responders *(men are to initiate the relationship)*

WHAT should they do?
1. Be Under a "Covering." This should be a person you respect and admire. Your spiritual covering should be an individual or couple whom you trust and whose wisdom and behavior is consistent with biblical principles (see chapter 3 for details).

2. Identify Timeless Traits. Think through the traits you desire to see in your potential mate. You probably already have a "list," but reexamine it to ensure that it does not contain just your personal preferences but that it is driven by biblical principles that make great marriages.

3. Introduce Your Covering. If someone approaches you, and you are interested, introduce that person to your spiritual father/spiritual parents. Your spiritual father/parent(s), or the couple you have identified as your mentor couple, might be able to point out potential flaws in the person's character that you are either blind to or have simply overlooked. Although you would never want to force a relationship, be aware that you should remain open to God bringing your mate in an unexpected package.

4. Observe Your Potential Mate. Observe the man to identify the timeless traits you are looking for. Measure him against your newly assessed list that includes the biblical principles God has defined for the male role. Ask the people in his sphere of influence questions related to his character. Include his friends, casual acquaintances, people he may not be so friendly with, family members, ministry leaders, and associates. You may be surprised what you can learn from people with whom he interacts. The idea is to gather information about his character, including how he interacts with people he doesn't necessary get along with. This will help you see if his good behavior is authentic or just merely a show! It's important not to discard or dismiss any negative sentiments you may receive from people about him. If you do encounter people with whom he has had difficulty relating, try to find out why and under what circumstances. We're not saying to take their opinions as law, but consider them within the context of your overall observations and what you are learning about his character.

5. Consult Your Covering. Continually meet with your spiritual father/parent(s) to monitor and discuss the steps you are undertaking, the progress of the relationship, and the emotions you are experiencing.

6. Make a Decision Together. After discussing the relationship with the man who is pursuing you, resist the desire to be exclusive too early. Be sure to include your mentor or covering, and, after much prayer and reflection, decide if you are strong enough as a couple to continue going forward. Remember, you can't have too much prayer! Make the decision whether or not to pursue a serious relationship that could lead to marriage.

7. Enter a Courtship. The agreement to become engaged should be initiated by the man. You should receive clear direction from him, and most important, make sure that you enjoy the experience! Remember, at this phase, for all intents and purposes, you are engaged. The formal proposal could come at any time.

8. Marriage. After you are married, the *real* work begins! Be sure you set aside extra time for a devotional quiet time with God as a couple. You're going to need it!

9. Continue to Meet with Your Mentor Couple. Regular meetings should be set up between couples. If and when problems arise, either you or your spouse should feel free to contact the mentor couple for help to resolve the issue in a godly manner.

Identifying Timeless Traits

Aaaaahhh. You were probably wondering when we were going to get to this part. This is where we discuss what goes on that "list" that you should use to measure the man or woman you're interested in. It is critical that a potential mate be able to hear and respond to God's direction in every area of life.

One of the key factors to achieving a successful marriage is becoming the right person. This is primarily done by developing spiritual maturity, which enhances the ability to identify the right mate. Applying the wisdom of God will guide you in your search. What characteristics do you look for? Often, singles look for people who complement them or people who they believe will help them have a better future, but they overlook the *timeless traits* that make a healthy marriage. People tend to get caught up in things that might change, such as physical appearance, financial status, professional careers, and educational background. Now don't get me wrong; these qualities aren't to be ignored completely, but they are definitely fleeting and won't serve as the bedrock of a lasting, healthy marriage.

The "list" has less to do with your personal preferences and more to do with what makes a healthy marriage. When searching for the right mate for Isaac, Abraham's servant looked for a young lady with a servant's heart. He identified a woman who was considerate enough to offer water to his animals (see Genesis 24). Not once did he ask God for her to be beautiful or to have a college degree. Likewise, we should prioritize a person's character over his/her outward appearance and trappings.

All It Takes Is F.A.I.T.H.

The word "faith" occurs more than 230 times in the New Testament. More than forty of those occurrences are direct words from Jesus. He is most impressed when people show faith in God. And Jesus often rebuked His disciples for their lack of it. Throughout the Bible, faith is directly related to healing, blessing, and salvation, whereas the lack of faith is directly related to doubt, worry, and fear. We use the word *faith* here as an acrostic for identifying lasting qualities in potential mates. Remember that everything you look for in someone else must be something you value within yourself. So first ask yourself, "Do I have F.A.I.T.H?"

F.A.I.T.H. is: **F**aithfulness, **A**wareness, **I**nitiative (for men), **I**ntentional responsiveness (for women), **T**eachability, and **H**umility before God. Over the next few pages, we'll discuss each of these characteristics in more detail.

Faithfulness *(Matthew 17:20)*

The quality of faithfulness is twofold. First, faithfulness relates to whether the person is a Christian. You cannot begin to assess how a person lives his life without the assurance that he or she has professed Christ as Savior and Lord. It is amazing how often singles try to skip this step and focus on all the "good" qualities a person may exhibit. However, all the goodness in the world is meaningless if a person is not a Christian—one who has received the eternal salvation that the Lord Jesus Christ afforded to those who believe in Him. Moreover, it is unfair and unbiblical to expect someone who isn't saved to consistently model the characteristics that are indicative of believers.

The second aspect of faithfulness has to do with a person's trustworthiness and dependability. You need to know if the person you're considering as a mate values commitment and integrity. A person's ability to stick with situations and keep his word, even when it's difficult, is a person who is ready to face some of the many challenges that will arise in marriage. Ask yourself if the person you're evaluating quits things before he/she finishes them. Does the person follow through on commitments and promises or is he/she known for being "flaky"—that is, one who exhibits inconsistent behavior?

Awareness *(Matthew 26:34–35)*

Have you ever been driving down the street and noticed a car with the gas caps off? Or maybe a person's seat belt or an article of clothing was dragging underneath the car door? Didn't you wish you could make the people aware of it so they could correct the situation? Awareness is the quality of understanding one's self. It means that the individual is clued in to his/her areas of weakness and strength.

Like the drivers with the dangling seat belts or open gas caps, we all have issues that others can readily observe. The question is whether we can recognize our own issues. When the desire is to present yourself as God's best, you should place priority on knowing who you are and who you are not, what you're great at, and what you struggle with. Expect the same from someone with whom you might enter a relationship. When a person is unaware of his/her true character traits or is dishonest about who he/she is, there is often blame placed on other people and circumstances for what happens in his/her life. Such people choose to ignore or deny their character flaws instead of taking personal responsibility for their choices and actions. As a result, they miss out on valuable opportunities for personal and spiritual growth.

People who lack self-awareness are usually clueless as to how their behavior affects those around them. In Matthew 26:34–35, Jesus told Peter that he would deny Him as Lord three times before the cock would crow. Peter, lacking self-awareness, adamantly denied this claim. Peter had such a distorted picture of himself that he actually argued against something that Jesus said was true! When we suffer from a lack of self-awareness, we may convince ourselves that we are better than we actually are. That prevents us from being able to grow in grace and become spiritually mature.

Initiative *(Matthew 9:2)*

By now you know that Jada and I believe men should never embrace a passive way of living. Life is too short and the call of Christ too great for us not to be initiative-takers. To clarify, men need to take the initiative in obedience to God's Word and not in fulfilling the desires of the flesh. That means that women should be looking to see if a man actively pursues Christ's plan for his life. She should also observe whether or not he takes the initiative in living for Christ through evangelism, service, and righteous living in general.

Does the prospective husband graciously yet firmly take on a leadership role, even if that means he's leading through serving? These are the things Christ asked us to do. Most men have no problem taking the initiative in their careers, education, and finances; but they should also be quick to serve others, resolve conflicts, or apologize when dealing with interpersonal relationships. *How* it's done may vary according to a man's personality, but *if* it's done is not even a question. Jesus said we are to make disciples, love our neighbors, and love God. Christ calls us to be active representatives for Him; we can't just wait for things to cross our paths or simply drop in our laps.

Ladies, of course, this also means that the man should take the lead role in finding a good wife as we are told in Proverbs 18:22. Therefore, it stands to reason that the man would take the initiative in pursuing dating relationships.

Intentionally Responsive *(Ephesians 5:33)*

If you want to know how a woman deals with authority, you need to observe how she responds to anyone in authority over her and also how she responds to other men. Does she have a kind attitude or a sharp response? Is she respectful to men or does she belittle them? How does she treat the authorities in her life? Men need to think seriously about this characteristic in a woman because it is the essence of submission. We're not talking about whether she's introverted or extroverted. *A note of caution:* Quiet or introverted personalities do not guarantee a submissive spirit. This is one of the most common mistakes men make. A woman's willingness to submit or respond to authority is demonstrated when she chooses to submit her opinions, decisions, and will to someone else *with a gracious attitude*. Whether it's with a girl-friend, a parent, co-worker, or potential husband, it's important to observe her *willingness* to relinquish control when it is important to do so, regardless of her *capability* to be in control.

Teachability *(Luke 8:25)*

Teachability is a characteristic that indicates a person's desire and ability to learn and continuously grow. It's the next step you take once you understand the concept of what it means to be aware. First, you know who you are; then you take steps to grow as you need to. Teachability and awareness go hand in hand.

In Luke 8:25 Jesus asked the disciples, "Where is your faith?" He had just spent most of the account in chapter 8 sharing wonderful parables and teaching His followers. Later in Luke 13:18–19 when He taught about the mustard seed, Jesus compared it to the amount of faith necessary to touch God. He explained that though it was one of the smallest seeds, it yielded one of the largest plants—up to twelve feet in height!

When a fierce storm arose and the disciples immediately became doubtful (Luke 8:25), they should have relied on what Jesus had just taught them—they did not demonstrate teachability. Their disappointing behavior led to Jesus questioning their lack of faith. Would they ever learn? Later on in Luke 17:5, the disciples asked Jesus to increase their faith. Once they had finally become aware of their issue, they became responsive and open to internalizing what Christ had to say. In other words, they were now prepared to receive from the Lord's teaching.

Flexibility is another aspect of teachability and is one of the most important elements involved in sustaining a healthy marriage. The opposite of flexibility is stubbornness or an unwillingness to move from one's position. It divides homes and destroys marriages. Stubbornness is rooted in self, but flexibility is rooted in love for God and for others. God's Word prompts us to put others' interests above our own (Philippians 2:3) and to love our neighbors as ourselves (Matthew 22:39). Is the person you're evaluating willing to change his or her opinion? Has that person shown he or she has the ability to learn from anyone and anything? Does that person always have to have his or her way, or does that person know how to choose battles wisely?

Humility Before God *(Matthew 23:12; Philippians 2:5–8)*

Humility before God is demonstrated by how people live out their spiritual lives on a daily basis. Merely observing a person's character and walk of faith during Sunday or Wednesday services cannot accurately assess that person's humility toward God. You need opportunities to see him/her in the mundane activities of life in order to observe the fruit from his or her relationship with Christ. Is he as passionate about pleasing Him as he is about achieving his own personal goals? Is she genuinely hurt when her actions disappoint Christ? Does he serve faithfully in kingdom ministry? Are pride and arrogance trademarks of her character? Acquiring answers to these questions can provide important insight into a person's spiritual life.

Humility before God, which comes only from having a heart for God, is an essential attribute for any future spouse to possess. Without it, you may find your life becoming as dry as the wilderness the Israelites wandered in for so many years because of their lack of humility and unyielding stubbornness. In Matthew 23:12, Jesus issued a strong warning that if we focus on being exalted, He will make sure we are humbled. On the other hand, if we humble ourselves in submission to God, He will make sure we are promoted. If Jesus sees humility as an important quality, then we should do no less.

Considering all of these traits, the significance of F.A.I.T.H. is evident when you're trying to recognize a potential mate. The point of looking for these traits in a person is not to have some legalistic checklist that you are using to disqualify people but to have some basic principles to identify in others that will help lay the foundation for a strong, healthy, dynamic marriage. But also remember, before you decide if a potential mate demonstrates these qualities; take a look in the mirror. Of course there will be some areas where you are stronger and some areas that will be challenging for you; this will also be true for the person you're evaluating. But the bottom line is, the individual who strives to live righteously must remove the log out of his or her own eye before addressing the speck in the eye of a brother or sister. And through it all—don't forget to keep the F.A.I.T.H.!

Beyond Traits . . . Looking Beneath the Surface

The more we've shared this F.A.I.T.H. principle in various venues, the more we've come to realize how some people can fake these qualities to some extent. We have met many men and women who have mastered the art of performing these five qualities. They seem to possess the attributes of faith, but when we, or a potential mate, take a deeper look beneath the surface, a different picture emerges.

We call this the "lemon principle." This happens when what you see on the outside doesn't always reflect an accurate picture of what's going on inside. This situation can be very dangerous. We call it the lemon principle because it's the same issue you may face when purchasing a used car. You need to know if what is found under the hood matches the sparkling exterior of the car. Truth be told, because of the condition of human nature, we are all used. But we don't have to be "lemons." Many newlyweds realize—after it's too late—that they didn't dig far enough beneath the surface and now find themselves feeling duped or deceived about the person whom they married.

Most of us would not buy a car solely based on how it looks, so why does that become so important when choosing the person with whom we will spend the rest of our lives? Where is the logic in this approach? If you're already in a premarital relationship and you want to avoid marrying a "lemon," consider this seven-point character inspection.

1. Do you have a mechanic? The *mechanic* in our analogy here represents a covering. The God of all creation fine-tuned the marriage union so that the husband and wife are taking two distinct actions. In Genesis 2:24 the King James Bible refers to these actions by saying they must "leave" their parents and "cleave" to each other. Ladies, you go from the covering of your parents (or spiritual parents) to the covering of your husband. Men, as the head of your household, you move from your spiritual covering and become your wife's covering. Does your potential mate have a spiritual covering? Who is assisting the two of you with making major decisions regarding your future marriage?

2. Do you know the history of the car? When you buy a used car, you usually want to know about any accidents the car has been in, as well as other "trouble areas" that may exist. Likewise, long before you walk down the aisle with a person, you need to know his or her history. This is not necessarily for judgment or disqualification, but it is important to know some vital information about your potential mate's background. For example, you will want to know if he or she has ever observed a successful marriage in her family history. Knowing about someone's past can make the difference in how you approach your relationship and can clue you in to challenges you could face in the future. Keep in mind that when you expect others to share about their history, it requires that you be accepting and affirming as they reveal the scars that possibly lie beneath the surface.

3. Does the relationship suffer from the ArmorAll complex? Have you ever walked into a used car dealership and been blinded by the shine of a car? All that gloss is sometimes just an attempt to hide the imperfections that exist. The seller wants you to be so overwhelmed with the car's external attributes that you don't even ask the important questions. First Chronicles 28:9 declares, "And you, Solomon my son, obey the God of your father and serve him with a submissive attitude and a willing spirit, for the Lord examines all minds and understands every motive of one's thoughts. If you seek him, he will let you find him, but if you abandon him, he will reject you permanently."

During the course of your relationship, have you asked the important questions? Or have you been so "taken" with his/her external attributes that you're oohing and aahing without noticing that black smoke is shooting out of the exhaust pipe? Be careful; even the best-applied ArmorAll washes off with the first rain.

4. Does he/she have a reliable dipstick? A mechanic uses a dipstick to determine the level of oil in a vehicle. The importance of oil in a car goes without saying—it preserves the life of the engine, the most important component inside a vehicle. In Matthew 12:34 Jesus said, "Offspring of vipers! How are you able to say anything good, since you are evil? For the mouth speaks from what fills the heart." Since the heart is the most vital component in a person, the dipstick being referred to here is the tongue. In relationships, the tongue is the dipstick, or instrument, that will show you what's in another person's heart. James 3:2 says, "For we all stumble in many ways. If someone does not stumble in what he says, he is a perfect individual, able to control the entire body as well." This is a biblical goal that Christians must earnestly strive to attain as we seek to please God in every aspect of our lives. Be alert and sensitive as you observe what is coming out of your potential mate's mouth. By simply listening to a person talk, you can learn a great deal about who he/she is.

5. Who has the keys? In inspection point 4, the statement was made that the heart was the most vital component of a person. The heart is to us what an engine is to a car. Without the keys, however, that car will not go anywhere. Placing the key into the ignition and turning it starts the engine and gets the car ready to drive. Just as you would not give your car keys to just anyone, and thereby give them access to drive your car, you need to be sure of who holds the keys to your potential mate's heart. Proverbs 4:23 exhorts us to "Guard your heart with all vigilance, for from it are the sources of life." You need to know if your potential mate has given the keys to his/her heart to anyone else. Is he/she still communicating with a special someone from a past relationship? If you don't know who has the keys, you may walk out of your front door one day and discover that the car you thought was in your driveway is gone.

6. Check your speed: How fast are you going? Philippians 4:6 declares, "Do not be anxious about anything. Instead, in every situation, through prayer and petition with thanksgiving, tell your requests to God." How fast are you moving in your relationship? Are you prayerfully moving toward marriage? While it is important to make sure you do all that you can to determine if this is the right mate for you, this process should not drag on for years and years.

You must remember that there are two hearts involved in this process. A person's heart was not designed to be "led on" for an undetermined period of time; neither should it be bonded to another without a definite commitment being made. Can we tell you how long the courtship or dating process should take? No. But we are saying that both of you should *clearly* and *honestly* communicate to each other your expectations so that hearts are not broken in the process. If you are too tough to be honest about your feelings, it will be impossible for the other person to make an accurate assessment of the emotional and spiritual temperature of the relationship. On the other hand, if you share your feelings and they are disregarded by the other person, this may be another sign to exit the situation.

7. Are the rims more valuable than the rest of the car? (Matthew 6:19–21) If you see a car that has accessories that are more valuable than the car itself, you may be looking at a lemon. Spending too much money on enhancements such as speakers, rims, radio systems, and the like doesn't make much sense if the same investment hasn't been made on the unseen aspects of the car such as the engine, transmission, or the air-conditioning. Why is this question important to consider? Money! Money! Money! This is one way to determine how your potential mate spends money. While financial status is not critical to a successful marriage, sound financial values are. A fight over money (how it's spent and/or the lack of it) is one of the top five reasons for divorces today. Does he or she value external things more than internal things? A nice new suit or a beautiful new dress is meaningless if there is no beauty or godly character underneath.

Okay, yet another checklist and more information. So what's a woman to do when a man has expressed interest? What is a man's next step once he becomes interested? Reread this chapter slowly, and rely on the F.A.I.T.H. principles to help you observe your potential mate. Most important, relax and let God speak to your heart. If you listen and obey, He will never lead you astray.

Seven

our story:
"he said, she said"

his side of the story

Several years ago I began observing a young lady in our church. She was working in our youth ministry as the youth worship leader and on the team of senior high teachers. She had devoted herself to ministry. When she was not working in either of those two areas, she was serving as worship leader for the young adult choir at our church. Somehow it seemed as if she was always in my presence. She knew nothing about me observing her, but I was. I was evaluating her. I was not simply looking for a girl-friend; I was looking for a life partner.

A year earlier I had decided, along with some of my friends from seminary, to pray for our future mates every week. We were asking God to send us women who loved God and exhibited high character. So for me, the question was not only a matter of her being attractive—which this young lady happened to be—it was a matter of character. I needed to know if she had the qualities necessary to build a strong family, a stable and healthy relationship, and a God-honoring future, no matter what the future might hold.

So I had to ask some questions: (1) Was she flexible? (2) Was she aware? (3) Was she intentionally submissive? (4) Was she teachable? (5) Did she demonstrate humility before God? These qualities are of paramount importance because they indicate whether someone will be a healthy mate; they were also the qualities Jesus looked for in the disciples He selected to change the world. In Matthew 4, Jesus found disciples who were faithful and flexible; they dropped what they were doing to follow Him. He found men who were aware; they knew they had encountered the one John the Baptist had preached about. They were also submissive and teachable, which was mandatory in order to "follow Him" as He commanded.

To continue my information gathering, I observed her as she interacted with her friends. Did she have more guy friends than girlfriends? Who were her mentors? What was the quality of the girls she hung out with? All these questions were important to me, and so I simply observed her to see whether I could get answers without engaging her heart. In order to do this, I had to pray and trust God to allow our paths to cross over the course of the next several months. I knew that it would have been very difficult to seek the answers to these questions objectively if I was falling in love with her at the same time that I was observing her. The worst thing I could have done was to engage her heart or get her emotions or my own involved. To prevent that from happening and to avoid another broken heart, I tried my best to pursue my observations her without her knowing it.

One problem I encountered early on was that all the stories I heard about her were glowing. It was all positive, but because I knew she was a human being, I knew she had to have some issues. So my next pursuit was to identify some enemies (see chapter 6 under the "Observe Your Potential Mate" step). I wanted to find some people who had worked with her and did not like her for one reason or the other. I needed to know what those reasons were and how she handled confrontation, keeping in mind my desire to try to discern her heart and character. What better way to discover her potential traits than to ask people who struggled when working with her? Now don't get me wrong. I was not looking for angry, self-absorbed individuals who simply wanted to "dump" on me about her. I was looking for patterns in behavior that could expose weaknesses in her character. Proverbs 22:1 highlights one of the most important things in life as being our name because it represents our reputation. From her enemies, I found out that she was committed to excellence, did not tolerate mediocrity, was articulate, talked a little too much, and had a quick tongue. That's what her enemies said. I took note and began examining those traits to see if they were true.

I must say that the thing I liked the most about her was that she was not looking for a mate; she was simply serving God and trying to have as much fun as she could. Actually, I later learned that Jada and her friends really thought that she would be the last of her friends to get married. That was appealing to me. She was a saint who was serving God and an attractive young lady with a tender heart for Him. I thought, *WOW!*

After I was about three quarters of the way through my observing process, I asked a friend of mine, who was the youth pastor of our church at the time, about Jada's service as a volunteer in the youth ministry. He had only great things to say about her. He confirmed many of my findings and answered some questions directly for me. However, he also told Jada prematurely that I liked her, and so I had to clarify my intentions quicker than I had planned. The last thing I wanted was for her to wonder or dream about some guy who she "heard" liked her. I had learned the hard way from the previous experience I described in chapter 1 how easily a woman's emotions can become engaged.

Because Jada was informed by my friend, the observation period had to end. I now had to clarify how this relationship would be different, and I had to begin protecting her heart by communicating a clear vision for the direction of our relationship. One day a mutual friend brought her over to the office. I then asked her if she minded giving me her phone number. She gave me her number, and about two weeks later I phoned her. I spent those weeks in prayer, seeking God and asking Him to lead and direct the relationship. Then I made the call and invited Jada to dinner. I had two reasons for having dinner with her. First, I needed to explain the situation that my friend had placed us in, and second, I needed to lay out a plan for our relationship.

I proceeded to follow the steps described in chapter 6, using them as a road map to give her direction and to provide accountability and guidance for me. At this point, the first four steps were already completed. I was under the covering of my father and two other mentors. I had identified and observed the timeless traits in her and was very satisfied with the results. My initial contact with her was made through a conversation generated by me. When I asked Jada to dinner, her heart was engaged as I shared my interest in establishing a relationship with her. Jada immediately began observing me after that evening.

At dinner we had a blast. Initially, it was a little awkward; I had a list of questions that I asked her based on the timeless traits. It was important to discern what she valued as an individual and as a Christian. We ended up having a five-hour conversation instead of a two-hour dinner. She was simply terrific. Many of my questions were answered and many of my concerns were addressed.

The primary goal was to clarify my intentions for the relationship. I had to set direction and lay the foundation upon which the relationship would rest. So I did the following six things: (1) I shared my philosophy on dating, courting, and marriage; (2) I apologized for not personally sharing my interest in her; (3) I shared I had taken the opportunity to observe her, but that I realized that she needed to observe me also; (4) I shared with her that she could have the time she needed, but that it would not be wise for that time frame to be indefinite. I also suggested that we build in various check-in points to determine where we stood with each other. (5) I shared my commitment to her as a woman of God and as a sister in Christ; and (6) I communicated my desire to ensure that she would grow closer to God because of this relationship. Finally, I would do my best to make sure that she was a better person because God allowed our paths to cross.

The following events describe in detail how we progressed through the remainder of our plan. As our relationship unfolded and flourished, we fulfilled the courtship, engagement, marriage, and subsequent meetings with our mentor couple.

The Trip to Israel

The relationship continued for weeks, and we got to know each other better. We went out on dates with other couples, we did ministry together, I met her friends, she met my friends, we asked the hard questions of each other's friends, and we heard fascinating anecdotes from each other's past. We decided that the relationship was progressing well, and it was time to make a decision as to whether we would enter a courtship period.

As a part of my seminary training I was given the opportunity to go to Israel. It was then that we decided to fast one day a week while we were apart for three weeks to discern if this was God's will for us. We concluded that at the end of my three weeks in Israel we would decide whether or not to become engaged. During this time we sought counsel, prayed, and read two books: *Saving Your Marriage Before It Starts* by Dr. Les Parrott III and Dr. Leslie Parrott, and *The Triumphant Marriage* by Dr. Neil Clark Warren. Our goal was to better understand what marriage was really all about, to begin evaluating how we felt about each other, and, most important, whether we were both ready for a lifetime commitment.

When I returned from Israel, it was evident to me that she was definitely the one for me. But I wondered what Jada was thinking. Would she feel the same way I felt? She picked me up at the airport, and we talked. She felt that God had been leading her in the same way. We were both overwhelmed with emotion by what we believed God was telling us. That was the day we made the decision to be married, and we entered the courtship phase. I told Jada that she did not have to worry about whether I would change my mind. I would not. I was making a commitment to God and to her. It was as good as if we were married. I was that confident in God and in who she was becoming as a woman of God.

The Permission

Once we decided to be married, I knew I had to talk to her father, who was her covering. So I set up a time to meet with him and ask permission to have his daughter's hand in marriage. We had an interesting and challenging conversation. Of course, her father wanted to know all about me and my plans for his daughter. He wanted to make sure I wasn't flaky or lazy. To assess my character, Mr. Cobon asked about my family background and listened carefully to my responses. He definitely did his job in protecting his daughter and making sure that she would only be given to a man who honored God and could protect her and provide for her. It was tough—as it should be—but in the end Jada's father honored my request and granted me permission to propose.

The Engagement

From the moment we entered into a courtship, I reminded Jada that I could ask her to marry me at any time. Confident in God, my character, and my leadership, she actually bought her wedding dress and began making plans because I had given her my word. I had not even bought her an engagement ring yet, but she could move forward with the necessary plans because we both knew how committed we were to God, to each other, and to a life together.

The day finally came. I bought the ring, and it was time to propose. I was nervous and scared, and I wondered if this was the right choice. Confident in God's Word and in Jada's character, I knew life with her would be better than life alone. So I had two good friends assist me in creating the ambiance for the proposal. The night was set with dozens of roses, a violin playing her favorite song, and a full moon. It was perfect. I proposed to her in her parents' backyard while her dad was inside without a clue as to what was going on. I felt pretty smooth.

We walked in to share the news with her dad, and to our surprise the doorbell rang. It was two of her best friends, who coincidentally came over to visit. She was shocked, and I was shocked. It was not planned, and I could not take credit for it. They were all elated, and we all celebrated together.

The Wedding

Our wedding day took place at the First Baptist Church in Dallas, Texas, which is known for its rich history and architecture. My mentor, pastor, and spiritual father officiated at the wedding. Our families were all present, and some of our best friends were standing with us. We wanted to prepare for life together, not just a wedding. As soon as I asked Jada to marry me, I requested that she read a book called *Inviting God to Your Wedding*, by Martha Williamson. It helps brides-to-be and grooms-to-be keep the right focus as they plan their nuptials.

We committed early on to making sure that our wedding day would be distinctively biblical and would celebrate God and His plan for salvation and sanctification. Our wedding was designed to model the reality of the return of Christ for His bride. We wanted a worship service, not just a wedding ceremony. Therefore, our dream wedding included an evangelistic appeal, not just an entertainment attraction. We planned it based on Revelation 19:7, which declares, "Let us rejoice and exult and give him glory, because the wedding celebration of the Lamb has come, and his bride has made herself ready." In this passage, the bride, Christ's church, is supposed to ready herself for the groom, Christ, when He returns. The principle of a man taking the initiative and "finding" his wife is also seen in this verse. It perfectly captures the essence of our union by reflecting the relationship between Christ and His bride. Most important, this backdrop created a great opportunity to present the gospel of Jesus Christ.

Planning for a Lifetime Together

One of the most powerful things any human being can have is a vision of the future. What will our marriage look like? What are our values? What is it that we are asking God to do in us and then through us? What are we involved in that will demand our staying on our knees as a couple and as a family? What are we doing that is bigger than ourselves and that will make a difference in this world? What legacy will we leave for our family and the generations to come?

During our courtship, these questions guided our discussions, and we created a manifesto, of sorts, that would give direction to our future family. It was a plan that would keep us from drifting; it was our hope that it would keep us focused and prevent us from allowing the world to determine our priorities. To achieve our vision and to ensure that we continually grow, Jada and I created annual goals in each of the following seven categories:

Emotional: *To be balanced emotionally means that you do not overreact or underreact in the midst of a crisis or when faced with a difficult situation. It also means not withholding or internalizing your emotions and not verbally responding in disgust or anger.*

Physical: *To be balanced physically means that you appreciate how you have been fearfully and wonderfully made. You recognize that your body is the temple of the Holy Spirit, and you take care of it by eating well, exercising consistently, getting enough sleep, and getting regular physical checkups.*

Financial: *To be balanced financially means that you are living below your means, not above them. You have a financial plan and follow the "give, save, spend" model of stewardship.*

Spiritual: *To be balanced spiritually means that you are consistently showing off God's glory with your life by living out the fruit of the Spirit in your relationships, growing, reaching out in evangelism, being connected to a small group of Christians, and being a good steward with the gifts and resources that God has given you.*

Professional: *To be balanced professionally means that you know what you do best and are committed to developing those God-given talents to their fullest potential.*

Personal: *To be balanced personally means that you ask and answer these questions: Who are you becoming in light of God's design for a man or woman? Whose image of manhood and womanhood are you following? What is your reputation? As a man, are you rejecting passivity, accepting responsibility, and loving sacrificially? As a woman, do you support and respect those in authority over you, empower and nurture those you come in contact with, relate to others with authentic connection, value the principle of a spiritual covering, and enhance the lives of others with your internal beauty?*

Relational: *To be balanced relationally means that you possess healthy same-sex relationships and that there are one, two, or three people whom you are willing to love sacrificially and are engaging in battle for their souls. It also means that when Conway must interact with the opposite sex, he will follow 1 Timothy 5:2 (AMP), and "Treat younger women like sisters—in all purity."*

For each of these areas we both have three or four personal goals that we try to accomplish each year. Today, we are still trusting God and trying our best to stay balanced in these areas. Although we are far from perfect, we have seen over and over again that honoring God in our relationship has been a significant foundation on which to build a healthy and rewarding marriage.

her side of the story

Several years ago I took a trip to New York City to visit Columbia University. I had decided to get an M.B.A. degree, and I wanted to get into a top school. Columbia was my last chance. I had taken the right test, filled out the right applications, and was focused on pursuing my degree. At that time I had been serving in the youth ministry at my church for about two years. I was heavily involved in working as a core team leader, teacher for the twelfth-grade Bible class, and worship leader for the youth praise team.

It was a very fulfilling and challenging time for me. The Lord was stretching me, and I was so excited to be immersed in ministry, but I was ready for a change of scenery; that's when I decided to pursue a graduate degree. While at Columbia University I visited the campus, met with an advisor, and imagined my life in New York. I just knew it would be awesome. I figured that was one of the benefits of being single—

having the freedom to move and change my life whenever I wanted.

In the following month of April I received a letter from Columbia. I quickly read through the traditional introductory language, "It was a pleasure meeting with you. . . . You seem to be a strong candidate. . . . However . . ." When I read "however," my eyes lingered there and my heart sank. I knew what was next. The letter said that I was being placed on a waiting list and would have priority in applying *next year.* I remember how defeated I felt. It was as if I wasn't smart enough, and my plans were failing. I asked God why He couldn't just let me get into school and move to New York. I sulked for the next several weeks.

About four weeks later, during early May, I was at church on a Wednesday night discussing some ministry issues with our youth pastor. During our conversation he abruptly interrupted. "Guess who likes you?" I groaned inside. A relationship was the furthest thing from my mind, and I couldn't think of anyone whom I might be interested in that he would even know, but I played along.

"Who?" I asked. His face lit up with excitement. "Conway Edwards!" he said.

"Who?" I asked again. I was still puzzled.

I had never heard that name before, and I thought I knew everybody at church. He went on to give me a passionate but awkward sales pitch about this Conway Edwards. He quickly told me how great Conway was. He told me that he was a seminarian, that he was on staff at the church, and that he planned to move to Jamaica someday to do full-time ministry. I was taken aback. Nothing in that description enticed me. After a couple of experiences I had sworn off seminarians because I assumed they were all stuffy, boring, and sheltered. I needed someone who was fun-loving, appreciated a free spirit, and lived a pretty laid-back life. That didn't describe any of the seminary students I knew. In addition to that, I certainly wasn't excited by a life of full-time ministry—especially in another country! That was an extraordinary résumé; it was enough for me to realize that whoever this guy was, he wasn't for me.

The next Sunday I realized who Conway was when I saw him at church for the first time. *How strange,* I thought. *This guy has been at the church for five years, and this is the first time I ever knew who he was.* I tried to wave at him, confident that he would wave back since he was interested in me, but he didn't respond. I lingered around a little to see if he would walk over and talk to me. After all, he liked me. But he didn't acknowledge me. He just kept socializing. I was a little irritated. My pride had gotten the best of me. *Oh, well,* I thought, *it doesn't matter anyway.*

A couple of weeks passed, and I was at church doing some ministry work with the youth pastor. He said, "Let's walk to the main building because this copier isn't working." I blindly followed him, and we wound up in Conway's cubicle. I'm sure I had the "deer in the headlights" look; I hated that awkward feeling. I felt like a schoolgirl playing silly games. I was never big on matchmaking, and suddenly I had become a victim. After standing at Conway's desk for seconds of silence that seemed like eternity, the youth pastor "mysteriously" had to leave and go do something. That left Conway and me alone making uncomfortable small talk. Finally, Conway said, "You know, I think you and I need to talk." I assumed he was alluding to the fact that I knew about his interest in me. He then said, "May I have your phone number so we can talk?" I proceeded to give him my number and then left there as soon as I could.

One day went by, and I received no phone call. Several days went by, and still no phone call. After one week passed I began to wonder if Conway would ever call. I wasn't even

sure why I cared, but for some reason I was actually antici-
pating hearing from him. Finally, after two weeks, Conway
called me at work one day. It was a conversation I'll never forget. This person I didn't even know began asking me some
pretty personal questions right away. He wanted to know
what I loved about ministry, who my close friends were, and
what women at the church I admired. I responded to all of his
questions, and he seemed satisfied with my answers.

He then apologized for how I had found out about his interest in me and suggested that we get together to discuss
the "confusion" that may have resulted. Then he suggested
we meet at the Cheesecake Factory! I was so thrilled that a
sheltered seminarian knew of a fun place to eat. In that one
conversation Conway set himself apart from any man I had
ever met. He was most interested in who I was as a person,
my ministry, and the people who influenced me. I was so re-
freshed and encouraged that if he and I had never spoken
again, I would have still been better for the conversation
alone. We set the dinner discussion for later in the week and
said good-bye.

The night for our discussion had finally arrived. I met
Conway at the restaurant at six that evening. I thought his
plan was to tell me that this was all a misunderstanding and
that we should probably just go our separate ways. My plan
was to "let him down easy." I was going to let him know that
I appreciated his interest, but this probably wouldn't work
out. After all, I wasn't remotely interested in a relationship at
the time.

Five hours later, at the request of the restaurant staff, we
left our table to finish talking outside. Conway had shared
that although he hadn't planned to tell me that he was interested in me until much later, he believed that God had divinely
allowed our paths to cross. He said God allowed us to meet
for one of three reasons: (1) to be friends for life; (2) to be

friends for a season; or (3) to be married. I thought, *Did he just say married?* Conway continued to explain his philosophy of relationships and marriage. He told me that he didn't believe in lengthy, drawn-out relationships and that "should I accept this mission" he would try his best to guard my heart. He said he had learned the hard way how precious a woman's heart was, and he wanted to do everything he could to protect mine.

Conway had dominated most of the conversation with prepared questions about me, my likes and dislikes, my family, and my values. He was trying to analyze me, but I refused to be figured out. So we played conversational chess. Both of us tried to ask questions that would provide insight about the other. I was absolutely impressed by his confidence and boldness as a Christian man, as well as the sharpness of his mind. As our discussion came to an end in the parking lot, Conway suggested that we not connect again for the next week but rather spend that time praying about what direction God might give us. I agreed, and we reluctantly parted ways. We were both surprised by how easily the conversation had flowed. As I drove home that night, I had to wonder if God was up to something.

Over the next week I received two very sweet cards from Conway, thanking me for the evening we had shared and reminding me that he was praying for me. Technically he had cheated and broken our agreement not to communicate for a week. But I was enamored. I remember telling my mom all about our night and showing her the two cards. She was excited for me, as moms always are.

The week came to an end, and Conway and I talked about what would become of our initial encounter. It didn't take long for us to both agree that God was definitely giving us the green light to move forward. He then laid out the next step in his "plan." It all seemed so formal. But the casual approach based on my past relationships hadn't worked at all, so I was open to how he wanted to proceed. He said that he wanted to give me some time to observe him and talk to his friends so I could make my own judgments.

It was then that I found out Conway had actually been observing me and a couple of other young ladies for almost a year. I was shocked. He told me that he would like to set a time when we would decide if the relationship was headed for marriage. It all happened pretty fast. I couldn't believe I was contemplating marrying someone I had known less than two months. I didn't think it was possible to come to such a serious decision in such a short time. Then the Lord spoke to my heart. He reminded me that all of my hesitancy was based on shallow desires and preferences, not on His principles. So I prayed about it and decided to go along with the plan.

Conway was taking a trip to Israel within the next few weeks and would be gone for about three weeks. I specifically remember that his return date was June 12, so that would be the date we would decide whether to move forward toward marriage. He and I talked enough while he was in Israel to rack up a good-sized phone bill. We started to discuss some pretty deep issues about what we wanted out of life and how we viewed marriage. He seriously discussed the possibility of living in Jamaica, and for some reason I felt an overwhelming ease about it. It wasn't anything like I had imagined it would be, but I knew that his confidence about our relationship was rooted in Christ. That fact made me comfortable in doing whatever he felt was best. We had decided to purchase journals before he left for Israel, and I was writing in mine every day. I was also counting the days until his return.

The day he came home, I went to the airport to pick him up. It was a tense morning. I already knew what God was confirming in my heart, and I was pretty sure Conway felt the same way. We engaged in small talk for a while as we headed toward home. After about five minutes of driving he said, "Pull the car over." I pulled over, and he looked me directly in my eyes and said, "I am certain that you are to be my wife." All I could say was, "Okay." He then said, "I'm ready to move forward." My heart was beating so fast; I couldn't believe what was happening. He seemed very calm, and we had just made a major life decision! We drove home chatting about everything in the world as if it were the most normal day of our lives.

From that point on, I knew that Conway could propose at any moment, so I figured it might be a good idea to let my dad know how serious this was. So a few days later I told my dad that Conway would be coming over for dinner to have a discussion with him. My dad had that wrinkled brow when he said, "About what?" I said, "Our relationship." I'm sure he was in denial, and that was the last thing he wanted to hear from his oldest daughter, so all I got from him was a grunt as he mumbled, "Okay. Whatever." We arranged for Conway to come over for dinner sometime during the last week of June. Dad didn't make it easy, but while he was in the backyard, Conway cornered him and asked for my hand in marriage. When they emerged from their outside chat, Conway looked calm and gave me the signal that everything had gone well. That was a miracle in itself! My dad wasn't an easy "sell," but Conway's character and my trust in him sealed the deal.

As our relationship progressed, we worked hard to maintain healthy boundaries and keep our emotions in check. Of course, it was difficult, but we constantly sought the Lord on how He would guide us. We read marriage preparation books and went through premarital counseling. I remember countless conversations wrestling with core issues that would affect our relationship. We discussed all our plans and desires with the Lord, and Conway brought amazing clarity to the courtship. During July and August we spent intentional time together learning about each other's lives. I got to see Conway's seminary life, met several of his friends, and asked their opinions about him. They all had great things to say. They loved his passion and enthusiasm and said he truly had a heart for God. I even got to hear about his weaknesses from a couple of very honest friends whom he trusted deeply.

In August, we headed to Jamaica to meet his family. I was nervous to be meeting my future in-laws, but they welcomed me with open arms. I felt even stronger about our future after seeing the godly foundation his parents had laid, and the Lord was already preparing my heart for living in Jamaica one day. By September, although Conway had not officially proposed, I began looking for a wedding dress and taking care of the major wedding details. Because we considered ourselves engaged, we had already set our wedding date. After a lot of searching, I found a beautiful church and a dress that fit me and my personality just perfectly.

My friends and family were quite skeptical about this whirlwind relationship. They couldn't believe that I had just met Conway less than five months earlier and things were moving so quickly. They also found it difficult at first to accept the fact that he was a student who wanted to pursue ministry in a third-world country. Moreover, they really couldn't understand why I was making wedding plans without having a ring on my finger. It just wasn't the way things were supposed to go. I told them repeatedly that if a piece of jewelry on my hand was more valuable than Conway's promise to marry me, which in essence was his word, we were in big trouble. Because of all of the resistance surrounding me, I felt very alone at times; however, I had every confidence that this was the right move for me. That time prepared me to be able to follow Conway's leadership even when others, including my own family, didn't agree. I tried to explain to them how God had changed so many of my insignificant preferences and had shown me the important principles that build a lasting marriage.

On a lovely October night, with a full moon brightly shining, my favorite hymn being played on a violin, dozens of red roses, and, of course—the element of surprise—Conway proposed. I accepted, and we were official.

We were married the following March, less than one year after I met him, and it continues to be an exciting and challenging ride. Apart from receiving salvation through Jesus Christ, marrying Conway was the best decision I have ever made in my entire life.

Concluding Thoughts: Your Stories

After reading our story, a number of thoughts may be running through your head. Ladies, you might be asking the Lord if a man is ever going to pursue you. Men, you might be asking Him if there is a woman out there for you or if you are really ready for such a commitment. We can't encourage you enough to accept the fact that God's standard does not waver on the subject of marriage. There really are no valid shortcuts. It is a most serious step in life that should be accomplished in God's own timing and in His way. We want you to know that God loves you, cherishes you, and wants you to thrive in your everyday life. He also desires to use you for His purposes. And know that time is truly of the essence.

Are we saying that you should put your feelings on the back burner and deny them? No, by all means, pray that God will send the individual for you according to His timetable. But until that happens, we want to challenge you to become involved in God's work and in doing what is pleasing to Him. Perhaps marriage is not in your immediate future. You even need to seriously consider the possibility that it may not be in your future at all. So if you delay taking risks for God and refrain from maximizing your gifts and resources for His glory, your delay is in vain. And you could be missing out on a tremendous blessing. God wants us to live for Him regardless of what we may be waiting on and what we think might make life complete.

Being single is not an excuse to feel sorry for yourself, or to feel as if you are not good enough to be married. The couples you see at church, in social settings, or leisurely walking by the lake constantly deal with some very heavy issues. A major part of the message we have attempted to convey through this book is that the issues in your life do not disappear when love finds you. Marriage is not a guarantee of happiness or joy—as Jada and I have realized—it is hard work.

So continue to hope and dream, but also begin to get involved, or further involved, in the plans that God has for you to serve Him in a local church. In this game of life there is always work for God's team to accomplish. Remember our Savior's words, "The harvest is plentiful, but the workers are few" (Matthew 9:37). It is our prayer that you will get off the sidelines, stop being a spectator, and get in the game. If you are one of those single Christians who stand on the wall at the club and/or surf the Net hoping for that chance to interact with the opposite sex, let it go! Trust God to bring your mate, and in the meantime busy yourself with serving Him.

As you read in our story, although we both wanted to be married someday, we made the decision as singles to allow God to have control in that area of our lives. We were also committed to serving Him faithfully until His perfect will became evident.

Eight

frequently
asked questions

Q1: *There's a guy who sits near me at church. We exchange friendly conversation from time to time during church and at singles events. I would like to converse with him more outside of these brief encounters just to get to know him better. If a woman is not to initiate interaction with a man, what options do I have in this situation?*

A1: It's usually not wise for a woman to initiate interaction with a man she's interested in. We would suggest that you pray about it. Ask God to reveal His will to both of you; and until He does, ask Him to help you control your emotions and desires for this man (no matter how trivial they may seem now). A godly man should understand God's order and will initiate communication if he is led to do so. Remember, men will go after what they want *when* they are ready. Philippians 4:6–7 tells us, "Do not be anxious about anything. Instead, in every situation, through prayer and petition with thanksgiving, tell your requests to God. And the peace of God that surpasses all understanding will guard your hearts and minds in Christ Jesus."

Q2: *How will a man know if the woman he is interested in is interested in him? From what I have heard, observation is a part of the process. But what if I spend two or three months observing, but never really engaging her in any conversation, and it turns out she doesn't want to pursue a relationship with me? Should I consider that wasted time?*

A2: Proverbs 3:5–6 tells us to "trust in the Lord with all your heart, and do not rely on your own understanding. Acknowledge him in all your ways, and he will make your paths straight." Based on the Word of God in these verses, we would say: (1) Do not rely on your own judgment alone; (2) ask God for guidance; (3) consider finding out more about her from trustworthy sources, for example, a mutual friend or someone who knows her but won't inform her that you have inquired about her; (4) consider talking with her directly to get an indication of her initial reaction to you. Note that merely talking to a woman is not considered engaging her heart. It's what you say and how you say it that can cause her heart to be engaged; and (5) remember that if your motives and intentions are pure, there is no such thing as wasted time. Even if a woman you observe is not interested in you, you will still benefit from practicing this selfless principle and trying your best to honor God in the process.

Q3: *Is it wrong for a woman to propose?*

A3: First Corinthians 14:40 reads, "And do everything in a decent and orderly manner." Proverbs 18:22 reads, "The one who finds a wife finds what is enjoyable, and receives a pleasurable gift from the Lord." It is very important that you remember to wait on God. In addition, a woman proposing to a man is the most obvious sign of initiation there is! Do you really want to marry a man who didn't ask you to be his wife? You are a precious, special gift for the man who has the boldness and confidence in Christ to initiate the engagement process with you. One of the dangers of a woman proposing to a man is that it automatically reverses the roles of the man and woman involved, and this issue is likely to cross over into marriage.

Q4: *How does a single person protect his or her heart?*

A4: Keep in mind that there are both verbal and nonverbal forms of engaging the heart. Verbal forms include: a) having deep discussions where emotions, vulnerabilities, and innermost feelings are shared or revealed, or b) when flirtatious words or thoughts are expressed, and when sexual or physical desires are expressed. Nonverbal forms include: a) extended eye contact, b) winking, c) physical touch, such as rubbing, massaging, and hugging.

Of course, more obvious nonverbal forms are kissing and being physically intimate. You can protect your heart by being aware of your own emotions when engaging in these and other verbal and nonverbal behaviors. Moreover, the behaviors mentioned above are not all-inclusive. Ask God to sharpen your self-awareness so that you are better able to discern what behaviors can trigger or engage your heart. Be honest with yourself. Setting appropriate boundaries is critical to successfully protecting your heart.

Q5: *Christian dating seems too difficult. I've pretty much chosen not to date at all. I wish we could just have friends of the opposite sex to hang out with from time to time, but I know from experience that doesn't work. What's a girl to do?*

A5: Galatians 6:9 reminds us, "We must not grow weary in doing good, for in due time we will reap, if we do not give up." Above all, please stay encouraged and remember that Christian dating/courtship does require discipline, just like the Christian walk itself. One of Satan's biggest traps is to deceive us into thinking that doing anything God's way is either too difficult, impossible, or doesn't consider our best interests. While Christian dating is not always easy, it is undoubtedly the most rewarding. Here's why:

(1) God is at the center of our focus. Society tells us to focus on ourselves, our interests, and how the person we are dating can meet our needs. (2) We learn some key disciplines that will equip us to be godly husbands and wives. (3) We assist each other in our Christian walk instead of causing each other to stumble. When a man and woman are operating in true Christian dating/courtship they value their relationship as a brother and sister in Christ. That allows them to inspire and encourage each other to grow in their Christian walk. This is the kind of relationship that can be beneficial to both people involved, even if it doesn't end in marriage. (4) We show God that we believe and have faith in Him. It's amazing how singles can trust God with all areas of their lives except in the area of dating and courtship. How much do we really love God? Do we love Him enough to give ourselves completely to Him? First Thessalonians 4:3–4 tells us that sexual purity is God's will for us. For a single person, that is the ultimate act of faith. And as for all Christians, single believers must be about the business of pleasing God by demonstrating faith in His abilities to supply *all* of their needs.

Q6: *Why does it seem that many Christian men prefer not to court the Christian ladies in their own church?*

A6: A lot of factors contribute to this issue. There is always an added set of pressures for a man to both approach and court a woman who attends his church. Some men feel uncomfortable because they feel that every move they make is being watched, and that they may be perceived as not having a true spiritual focus or motive. Other men fear the potential consequences that may result from being rejected in their church environment. For example, if a man approaches a woman at a mall and gets rejected, he most likely will never see her again. However, if a man gets rejected at his own church, he will be reminded of it every time he sees her at church.

Consider the pressure of being rejected by one woman only to try again by approaching another, and unfortunately being rejected again. If a man is not careful with his judgment, he could very easily become labeled as a womanizer, a player, or just someone who is not focused on true fellowship. There are some men who are intimidated or hesitant to approach a woman who is consistently "chatting with her girls" before and after church services. This setting only intensifies the "I don't want to be perceived as a Mack-daddy" syndrome. Please don't misinterpret what we are saying here; a woman should not deliberately disassociate herself from fellowship with her girlfriends hoping that a man will approach her. The godly man whom God has for you will find a way to approach you—no matter what the barriers are.

Other men don't feel comfortable courting a woman who attends his own church because it creates a more intense level of accountability. Some women may be wondering, How does this prevent a man from approaching me? Well, think about it. A man who is not serious in his walk with the Lord might not feel totally comfortable approaching a woman he knows is very serious about her Christian walk (based on having observed her demonstration of such traits in her service and interactions at church).

Q7: *I need help with the concept of "Christian dating." I have found many Christian men who are just as superficial as non-Christian men. It seems they want to put you through all types of tests before they even attempt to engage your mind, much less your heart. By the time I have reached the point where a man wants to engage my heart, I'm wiped out. I have no more to give. This is why I don't date. It takes a lot of effort to be considerate of another person and try your best to relate to him, only to realize he was trying to see if you would pass some test.*

A7: Both single men and women in churches around the country often have this perception about each other. Remember, just because a man goes to church does not mean he is living by the Word of God. In every church there is a broad spectrum of people. Some regular churchgoers aren't even Christians, while some walk closely with God and have given Him control over every aspect of their lives. This is why it is so important to observe people and their interactions at church. You'd be surprised at how much you can learn about a person and his or her level of spiritual focus just by watching that person.

It is also important to make sure you represent what it is that you want to attract. Since you aren't dating right now, use this time to work on yourself, and in God's timing He'll send the right man to you. Please don't be discouraged. It is admirable of you to have allowed yourself to trust Christian dating instead of worldly dating. But while you are waiting, please understand that not all Christian men are superficial. It only takes meeting that one real man of God for your life to be changed and blessed with a godly marriage. So don't allow your past experiences with the wrong men to distort what you know about God and what He can do for you. Allow the Word of God to constantly remind you, "I am able to do all things through the one who strengthens me" (Philippians 4:13).

Q8: *Why does God allow us to have urges that we can't control—in other words, natural, strong desires—knowing we can't do anything about it while single? I've prayed those urges away, but I still get them often. I do monitor who I'm around, what I watch, and what I listen to, and I stay in the Word, in church, and in constant prayer.*

A8: First Thessalonians 4:1–8 contends that purity is God's will for His people. First Corinthians 6:13–20 informs us that (1) we are to flee fornication; (2) we are not our own; and (3) we were bought with a price. The urges we have were never intended to be acted on in our single life. They are meant to be used only within the context of marriage. Satan wants us to believe that we can't control the urges we have. However, the fact that God commands us not to act on them also confirms that we do have the power to control them. We know this because God never gives us a command without giving us the strength or a way to follow it.

Has a man really and truly ever controlled his urges?

Yes. One of the best illustrations of this can be found in the book of Job. In Job 1:8, God describes Job as a blameless and upright man. Later in Job 31:1, Job states that he made a covenant with his eyes not to look lustfully at a girl. You see, Job himself was just a man who made a covenant not to allow lust to rule his life.

We too have the power within us through the Holy Spirit to control urges. But it begins with taking the following steps and maintaining them: (1) Be persistent in asking God for help to control the urges. We ask God for everything else. Why not ask Him to remove the spirit of sexual immorality from us? Some of us allow the guilt from past failures to interfere with our comfort level of asking God for help in this matter. (2) Make a promise to God to remain sexually pure at all costs. In Luke 9:23 Jesus said, "If anyone wants to become my follower, he must deny himself, take up his cross daily, and follow me." To follow Christ as a single means it will cost you your sexual desires and urges. It is a daily battle that one must fight in order to please Him. (3) Look at all people the way Christ sees them. Men should look at women as their sisters in Christ, not as sex objects. Women should look at men as brothers in Christ. If you are dating someone, your focus should be on interacting with the individual based on the Word of God and not on the will of your own selfish desires.

Q9: *Who is a spiritual father? What are the characteristics of a good spiritual father? Why do I need one?*

A9: In Psalm 128, the psalmist describes the importance of a man and the tremendous impact he has on his family, church, and country. It is the role of the father to disciple his family with a Christ-centered worldview and to impress upon them sound Christian values. Therefore, the father's role is to provide wisdom and guidance about life, which certainly includes the selection process of a mate.

When a man or a woman does not have a father figure who is alive and present in their lives or who is a practicing Christian, ideally the church should take on the role of the father and act as a covering by guiding each member in spiritual matters. Since marriage is definitely a spiritual matter, the community of believers, that is, the church and its leaders, should act as fathers for single individuals (1 Corinthians 4:14–15; 1 Thessalonians 2:11–12).

A good spiritual father should first be a fully devoted follower of Jesus Christ (Matthew 22:37–40; 28:19–20). He should also make wise and spiritual decisions based on the Word of God (1 Corinthians 2:15). Finally, he should be a good role model in speech, in life, in love, and in faith (1 Timothy 4:12).

Here are three final things to remember. First, it's a good thing to have a mentor couple or spiritual parent(s). We are witnesses to the fact that a mentor couple can provide great insight for you on your journey of life and spiritual growth. Second, if you can't find good candidates in your church, ask God to show you other options. It is God's desire that single men and women have this covering, so He'll provide what you need. You will be surprised how He allows other family members or father figures to step forward. Lastly, a woman should try her best to ensure there are no unhealthy emotions between her and the man she chooses as a spiritual father. If the two of you have anything other than a familial type of relationship, such as a brother/sister, father/daughter, or uncle/niece—just move on! Avoid the drama!

Q10: *If women should not initiate relationships with men, why was it acceptable for Ruth to initiate with Boaz (Ruth 3:6–9)?*

A10: Sometimes, women use Ruth's story to justify their initiation in relationships. However, a closer look at the context reveals the true meaning of Ruth's actions. Ruth's situation was a unique one. To understand her actions, you must first understand her cultural context. Ruth was a widow, and according to the law of her day, the responsibility of providing for widows was extended to the next of kin—usually a brother. If there was no brother to raise the children and provide for the widow, the responsibility of provision was passed to the next closest relative. The law also required the initiative of the widow in seeking marriage since widows were not obligated to remarry. Although Boaz was not Ruth's closest relative, he was recommended by Naomi, her mother-in-law. So in this case, Ruth was being obedient to her covering, Naomi, and to the law.

Q11: *What do I do if I'm already in a relationship but I now see that we need to step back and reevaluate it or maybe even end it?*

A11: If the person you're in a relationship with is a non-Christian, an unbeliever, you should graciously—yet firmly—end the relationship. Leaving no room for doubt, let the person know (without guilt, judgment, or an ultimatum) that you cannot allow the relationship to compromise your faith. Remember, we should never be bound to unbelievers (2 Corinthians 6:14).

On the other hand, the person may be a Christian, but you realize there are some delicate issues at hand. You should take a few days to seek God through prayer.

Allow your mind, heart, and emotions to all get on the same page so you can think as objectively as possible. Relationship issues often don't have cut-and-dried solutions, and you want to make sure you handle the situation with care. You should also consult your spiritual father or mentor for wisdom on how to proceed.

Your decision may be to either end or continue the relationship for the following reasons. First, you may decide to end the relationship for a number of reasons. If this is the case, make sure you clearly communicate with the other person, and let him or her know why you are ending the relationship. It's not wise to get into specifics because it may tempt the other person to change or conform to your request just to stay in the relationship. For example, it's safe to let him/her know that the relationship is unhealthy for you because you believe it is spiritually, emotionally, or physically unhealthy.

Second, you may decide to stay in the relationship with a mutual agreement to make the relationship healthier by taking some action such as pursuing counseling or meeting with a mentor or couple. In this case, after seeking God in prayer and talking with your spiritual advisors, share your concerns with the person you're in a relationship with. Let him/her know your thoughts and your suggested resolutions. Be open to his or her thoughts and feelings, and be willing to have authentic, maybe even painful, dialogue to reach an agreement without comprising your principles.

Most important, whenever you are ending a relationship or raising issues that need answers, remember to always take responsibility for your role in the demise or misdirection of the relationship. Whether you are a man or a woman, there is usually a boundary you didn't set plainly, a principle you didn't prioritize, or communication you didn't provide that could have contributed to the problems in the relationship. When it's all said and done, people should leave relationships with their heart and emotions intact. Not that there won't be pain or hurt—but there should not be permanent damage.

about
the authors

Conway Z. C. Edwards

Dr. Conway Edwards is the Singles Ministry Director and Pastoral Assistant to Dr. Anthony T. Evans, the Senior Pastor at Oak Cliff Bible Fellowship (OCBF) in Dallas, Texas. He was previously the Director of Spiritual Formation at OCBF, a position he held for three years. Conway also served as a leadership fellow at Dallas Theological Seminary in the Center for Christian Leadership, under the leadership of Dr. Howard Hendricks.

Under Conway's leadership, the singles ministry at Oak Cliff Bible Fellowship has grown in a year and a half from an average of thirty-five singles to over seven hundred in small groups and over five hundred attending monthly singles gatherings. The ministry has been marked by creativity, a commitment to excellence, volunteer involvement, and most important—a genuine desire to live for God.

Conway received his Master of Theology degree with an emphasis in Pastoral Leadership from Dallas Theological Seminary. He received his Doctor of Strategic Leadership from Regent University in Virginia. Conway also holds a Master of Business Administration with an emphasis in Human Resources. He teaches in the field of leadership and consults in leadership on a part-time basis for many churches and conferences across the United States and Jamaica. Some of the churches include Grace Church of Glendora in Glendora, California; Pinon Hills Community Church in Farmington, New Mexico; St. Luke Baptist Church in Little Rock, Arkansas; and New Faith Church in Houston, Texas. Some of the conferences that he directs include the Iron Sharpens Iron Leadership Conference in Dubuque, Iowa; The Urban Alternative's Church Development Conference in Dallas, Texas; and the National Centre for Christian Leadership Mentoring Conferences in Jamaica.

Conway is the Executive Director for the U.S.-based ministry Caribbean Choice for Christ, a ministry that seeks to train and develop leaders to infuse their institutions and communities with the gospel of Jesus Christ. He is also the Founder and President of the Jamaica-based National Centre for Christian Leadership-Jamaica (NCCLJ). These nonprofit organizations specialize in leadership consulting and leadership development and seek to equip leaders with biblically based strategies for effective church, civic, and professional leadership. Conway's desire is to see God bring forth 52,000 male Christian leaders on the island of Jamaica who understand their calling and are impacting their communities with a Christ-centered worldview.

Jamaica is Conway's original home. Discipling men and developing leaders are his passions. He firmly believes in and spends much of his time embracing the 2 Timothy 2:2 charge of mentoring and discipling other men.

Jada A. Edwards

Jada Edwards is the Process Analyst for the Dallas County Community College District (DCCCD) with over 55,000 enrolled students and eight educational campuses throughout Dallas County. Jada holds a Master of Business Administration with an emphasis in Organizational Strategy and has experience in improving organizations through process improvement and technological initiatives. She works in new business development, partner relations, and marketing for Caribbean Choice for Christ, a U.S.-based non-profit leadership organization, founded by her husband, Conway. Their ministry focuses on developing and equipping Christian leaders all over the United States and Jamaica.

An experienced speaker, Bible teacher, and mentor, Jada has committed her life to equipping women of all ages, regardless of marital status, with practical, biblical truth to help them live more genuine lives. She has served in various directional capacities within the youth and singles ministries at Oak Cliff Bible Fellowship, a church having over 1,000 youth and 3,000 singles. Jada currently resides in Dallas, Texas, with her husband, Conway.

discussion guide

Preface — Take the Lead

1. What does it look like for a man to lead with humility yet provide "certainty and security" in expressing his vision?

2. What does it mean for a man to provide a woman with security in the worldly sense? What does it mean in the biblical sense? Do the two ever overlap?

3. As a woman enters into a relationship with a man, should she be expected to give up certain things, such as professional goals, dreams, ministry work, independence, etc.?

4. What does sound, effective leadership look like?

Chapter 1 — The Journey Begins

1. How do I know I'm not justifying my decision with God's leading? How do I know it is or is not God?

2. I understand that it's important to "know myself, (and) know who I am becoming," but how do I do that? Where do I begin?

3. How can we recognize the difference between God's leading and our own overwhelming desire to achieve something?

4. It is critically important for men and women to be aware of who they are and who they are becoming. How does that process of awareness begin? How can a man or woman assess their level of self-awareness? Who should they turn to for guidance in this process?

Chapter 2 — The Man You Are Becoming

1. How do I know I'm not justifying my decision with God's leading? How do I know it is or is not God?

2. I understand it's important to "know myself, (and) know who I am becoming," but how do I do that? Where do I begin?

Chapter 3 — The Woman You Are Becoming

1. How do I know I'm not justifying my decision with God's leading? How do I know it is or is not God?

2. I understand it's important to "know myself, (and) know who I am becoming," but how do I do that? Where do I begin?

Chapter 4 — Who's Your Comforter?

1. Is it bad to surround oneself with people who make the individual feel secure and comforted at all times?

2. Is God really enough in all aspects of life? What situations arise in life that continually cause you to stumble? In these situations, who or what do you turn to for comfort?

3. What are healthy ways to deal with loneliness, frustration, insecurity, confusion. and anger?

4. What are productive ways to approach stress and boredom?

5. Is there anything wrong with wanting to be in a love relationship? How does a man or woman find contentment and purpose in singlehood? How does someone stop viewing singlehood as a never-ending season in life?

6. Are some people called to be single? Why or why not?

7. What does a life characterized by contentment look like?

8. Can someone be content with his or her life and still be ambitious? Is ambition a negative attribute?

9. How do we recognize God's timing and perfect will?

10. Is disappointment over circumstances a sign of discontentment? Why or why not?

Chapter 5 — Experiencing Healthy Relationships

1. How does one learn to have meaningful long-term relationships?

2. How does one deal with trust issues that hinder from having meaningful relationships?

3. What do someone's same-sex friendships reveal about how he/she will function in relationships with the opposite sex?

4. What is the best way for a man or a woman to "observe" or "evaluate" another person? How does a man or a woman avoid being distracted by the things that attract him or her to the individual?

5. Why is accountability important in same-sex friendships? How is accountability established and maintained? Is it unhealthy for male and female friends to be accountable to each other? Why or why not?

6. What does it look like to be consumed by God?

Chapter 6 — Got F.A.I.T.H.?

1. *What to Do* . . . When a man or woman makes a decision to "hold out" for God's chosen one, he/she at times can feel as if good options are always passing him or her by. While a man or woman doesn't want to lower his/her standards, a fear settles in that one may ultimately be alone. How does someone know if his or her standards are too high? How does someone know if he or she is settling for less?

2. What are some telltale signs that a person is a phony rather than the real deal?

3. How important is it that both partners are virgins? What if neither are or only one is?

4. How is the dating relationship/courtship altered for single parents? When and how do you introduce/involve the child(ren) in the relationship?

5. At what point does the relationship become an exclusively committed relationship?

6. At what point does an emotional investment in a relationship shift to engaging the heart? How do you guard against such a shift?

7. Is there a set timeline for a courting relationship? If yes, how and by whom is it set? If no, how should the couple go about determining what is best for their relationship?

8. How does a couple identify the "ideal mentor couple"? How does this relationship work, and how long does it last?

9. Is it wrong to have a list of expectations for a potential mate? Why or why not?

Chapter 7 — Our Story: "He Said, She Said"

1. The book suggests that men and women should be self-aware. How can a person who lacks self-awareness develop in that area?

2. Is teachability synonymous with obedience? How are the two alike? How are they different?

3. Is it appropriate for a woman to observe a man before the man has stated that he wants to pursue her?

4. In pursuing Jada, Conway made it a priority to find out more about her by talking to people who disliked her. Why is this beneficial? How should this information be evaluated considering an individual may have changed drastically since interacting with the people who disliked her?

5. If a man has begun actively pursuing a woman and has a list of questions for her, when and how should he pose those questions? Should the questions come all at once or over a period of time? Is the woman expected to answer all questions immediately, or can she answer them at a later date? When should questions of intimacy be posed and answered?

6. What is meant in the book by "check-in points" during his/her observation? Why is this essential to do?

7. If a woman is being observed for a future relationship, how is she then also viewed as a sister in Christ? How does a man's interaction with a woman change when he begins pursuing her? Should it change? Why or why not?

8. At what point during the courtship should the man meet the woman's family? And when should the woman meet his family?

9. What discussions, decisions, and plans should a couple start making together as they prepare for marriage; that is, choosing a home, joint finances, family planning, etc.?

Chapter 8 — Frequently Asked Questions

1. Is it possible that being nice can be mistaken for flirting? What are some of the differences between the two? How can the habit of flirting be broken? Avoided?

2. Is it ever appropriate for a woman to share intimate/personal information about herself with her closest male friends? Why or why not?

3. "Just because a man goes to church doesn't mean he is living by the Word of God." What type of behavior(s) should a man living by the Word exhibit? What are some indicators that a man is being authentic rather than "performing"?

4. If a woman has developed a distorted view of men based on past experiences, what can she do to correct that view, other than seek counseling?

5. *What to Do* . . . A woman meets a man who is a Christian, attends church, is active in ministry, reads and studies the Word; but he still has habits of the world such as drinking and cursing (neither in abundance). Are these habits absolute "deal breakers" in pursuing a relationship or just flaws? Should this woman walk with him through these issues? Why or why not?

6. What are some examples of information that *is* and *is not* appropriate to share with your spiritual father?

7. How do you know if your covering is truly living righteously?

8. How involved should spiritual fathers be in the lives of their spiritual sons and/or daughters? Should spiritual fathers be involved in all areas of their lives or focus primarily on the relationships they are involved in?

9. Should a woman's spiritual covering be married? Why or why not? What does the relationship look like between the wife and the covered woman?

10. How should a woman respond if she is approached by two men?

11. How does a woman recognize the man God has called to be her husband?

12. Would it be appropriate for a woman to share the information she has learned from this book with the man who has been pursuing her? In sharing this information with him, would she be functioning as a helpmate or would she be taking the lead?

13. How should a man or woman approach/engage in a relationship with someone who has been divorced?

14. If a friend is attempting to "hook you up" or wants to set you up on a blind date, should you participate in this? Why or why not?

15. If a woman has discovered that a man is observing her, but he has not yet made a decision to pursue her, how is she to respond to and interact with him from that point on if she is interested in him?

For booking information, questions, or comments,
write to us at:

When Love's in View
P.O. Box 223743
Dallas, Texas 75222

Visit our website at:
www.conwayandjadaedwards.com

e-mail us at:
info@conwayandjadaedwards.com

For more information about our leadership
development ministry in the Caribbean, please visit:
www.caribbeanchoice.org

We'd love to hear from you!

suggested reading list

Boy Meets Girl by Joshua Harris

Define the Relationship: A Candid Look at Breaking Up, Making Up, and Dating Well by Jeramy Clark and Jerusha Clark

I Kissed Dating Goodbye by Joshua Harris

Inviting God to Your Wedding by Martha Williamson

Raising a Modern Day Knight by Robert Lewis

Saving Your Marriage Before It Starts by Dr. Les Parrott III and Dr. Leslie Parrott

Sex Is Not the Problem (Lust Is) by Joshua Harris

The Dating Trap by Martha Ruppert

The Triumphant Marriage by Dr. Neil Clark Warren

The Negro National Anthem

Lift every voice and sing
Till earth and heaven ring,
Ring with the harmonies of Liberty;
Let our rejoicing rise
High as the listening skies,
Let it resound loud as the rolling sea.
Sing a song full of the faith that the dark past has taught us,
Sing a song full of the hope that the present has brought us,
Facing the rising sun of our new day begun
Let us march on till victory is won.

So begins the Black National Anthem, by James Weldon Johnson in 1900. Lift Every Voice is the name of the joint imprint of The Institute for Black Family Development and Moody Publishers.

Our vision is to advance the cause of Christ through publishing African-American Christians who educate, edify, and disciple Christians in the church community through quality books written for African Americans.

Since 1988, The Institute for Black Family Development, a 501(c)(3) non-profit Christian organization, has been providing training and technical assistance for churches and Chrisitan organizations. The Institute for Black Family Development's goal is to become a premier trainer in leadership development, management and strategic planning for pastors, ministers, volunteers, executives and key staff members of churches and Christian organizations. To learn more about The Institute for Black Family Development write us at:

The Institute for Black Family Development
15151 Faust
Detroit, Michigan 48223

We hope you enjoy this book from Moody Publishers. Our goal is to provide high-quality, thought-provoking books and products that connect truth to your real needs and challenges. For more information on other books and products written and produced from a biblical perspective, go to www.moodypublishers.com or write to:

Moody Publishers/LEV
820 N. LaSalle Boulevard
Chicago, IL 60610
www.moodypublishers.com

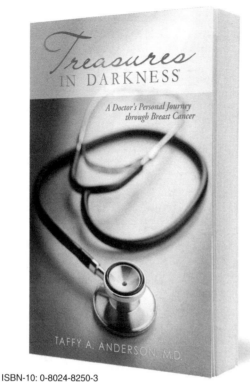

ISBN-10: 0-8024-8250-3
ISBN-13: 978-0-8024-8250-1

And I will give you the treasures of darkness and hidden riches of secret places

~ Isaiah 45:3

In this inspiring, true story, Dr. Taffy Anderson illuminates the treasures of darkness she gathered while fighting—and surviving—breast cancer. Both a medical and spiritual journal of her experience, *Treasures in Darkness* traces her journey from a busy OB/GYN at a major medical hospital who learns of her older sister's diagnosis with breast cancer, to her own shocking diagnosis three years later, through painful surgery, chemo treatments, and coming face-to-face with death. Along the way, she learns to submit to the sovereign will of God, draw strength from his presence and cherish each day of life.

by Taffy A. Anderson

Find it now at your favorite local or online bookstore.

www.LiftEveryVoiceBooks.com

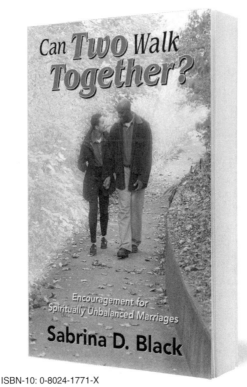

ISBN-10: 0-8024-1771-X
ISBN-13: 978-0-8024-1771-8

Find spiritual balance in your marriage

Many Christians are in spiritually unbalanced marriages, desperate for someone to minister to them in their unique place. This is a wonderful tool to provide those in unequally yoked relationships with hope and help in dealing with disappointment, hurts, and heartaches. Sabrina Black brings her counseling expertise to bear on this difficult subject, assisting couples with creating and maintaining a vibrant, growing relationship despite their differences. The *Can Two Walk Together Bible Study* is an excellent tool to help couples put offered guidance into practice.

Can Two Walk Together Bible Study ISBN-10: 0-8024-1772-8   ISBN-13: 978-0-8024-1772-5

by Sabrina D. Black

Find it now at your favorite local or online bookstore.

www.LiftEveryVoiceBooks.com

ISBN-10: 0-8024-8250-3
ISBN-13: 978-0-8024-8250-1

"Many young people believe Michael Bolton was the first artist to sing 'When a Man Loves a Woman' but actually it was written, produced and recorded by two others before Michael was born. Percy Sledge arranged the familiar tune in 1966, but Jacob of the Old Testament penned the first version in Genesis, chapter 29. Everyone knows that Jacob of the Old Testament was a rascal, usurper, and deceiver. But Jacob knew how to do one thing very well… Jacob knew how to love a woman. If you want to know if a man really loves a woman, take a close look at what Jacob has to tell us from the passages of Scripture."

by James Ford, Jr.

Find it now at your favorite local or online bookstore.

www.LiftEveryVoiceBooks.com